# SPOCK ON SPOCK

# SPOCK

*a memoir of growing up*

# ON

*with the century*

# SPOCK

BENJAMIN SPOCK, M.D., & MARY MORGAN

PANTHEON BOOKS · NEW YORK

All rights reserved under International and Pan-Americ
Copyright Conventions. Published in the United States by Pa.
theon Books, a division of Random House, Inc., New York, an
simultaneously in Canada by Random House of Canada Limited
Toronto.

Library of Congress Cataloging-in-Publication Data
Spock, Benjamin, 1903–
    Spock on Spock : a memoir of growing up with the century
/ Benjamin Spock ; recorded and edited by Mary Morgan ;
illustrated with black & white photographs throughout.
        p.     cm.
    Includes index.
    ISBN 0-394-57813-9
    1. Spock, Benjamin, 1903–   . 2. Pediatricians—United
States—Biography.   I. Morgan, Mary, 1943–   . II. Title.
RJ43.S64A3   1989
618.92'00092—dc20
[B]                                                        89-42645

*Permission acknowledgments and photo credits can be found
on page 273.*

MANUFACTURED IN THE UNITED STATES OF AMERICA

*For Mike Woodbury, M.D., who has heard
these stories many times*

# Preface

What made me fall in love with Ben Spock, the first time I saw him, was his way of telling a story. It wasn't long before I started collecting his stories on tape. Every time he began one of his amusing tales, I would yell, "Wait!" and run to get the tape recorder. After deciding to organize these stories into a book, I started out every morning with such enthusiasm that I could hardly wait to get up and shove a microphone under Ben's nose. Until I'd done my two or three hours of interviewing, he wasn't even allowed to go to the bathroom. I became so involved that I wanted to know more and more, so my probing went deeper. That's when the stories began to turn into a single story even more telling—the meaning of Ben's life as he sees it.

What was my purpose when I expanded this project? I wanted to be sure that Ben had some say in how history would remember him, and that his courageous political life would not be overshadowed by his more benign pediatric career. This possibility first came to mind several years ago when I visited an elementary school in Arkansas on Martin Luther King Day. I was amazed—and shocked—to hear Dr. King portrayed just as a kindly Sunday school teacher. His political life and activities, his outrage at racial injustice, his acts of civil disobedience were being quietly buried.

The world knows Benjamin Spock as a wonderful pediatrician and a wise one. Look up his name in an encyclopedia today and you'll find several glowing paragraphs about his work in child care; the final sentence will say he ran for president in 1972. His contributions to child care are essential parts of his achievement, but no less so is his political courage, his work in the disarmament movement, his nights in jail and days in court, the fences he has climbed in hopes of bringing the world justice and peace. They are all parts of his legacy, and it's important to have his own accounts of them recorded in his voice. The stories in this book come from all his moods—humorous and solemn, aggressive and shy, modest, and boastful; they mark setbacks as well as victories. Diving into Ben's past eighty-six years and collecting these stories has been one of the most thrilling endeavors of our lives, and an unexpectedly challenging one.

Literary collaboration can be a hazardous, uncharted course, especially between husband and wife. In this case it brought out the competitiveness in both of us. Many times we fought over details and directions; when I asked questions that Ben didn't want to answer, he would demand, "Whose book is this, anyhow?" But the effort ended by strengthening our essential compatibility and mutual respect. Not just here on the boat in Tortola but in Maine, California, and everywhere in between, we filled fifty tapes and read and edited the transcripts, which generated even more questions. Originally I had planned that the book should take the form of interviews. But as it developed, my questions and Ben's answers were merged into Ben's narrative, which reflects and makes visible the depth of both.

Ben's complete recall of the details of his life has made all of this possible. Like most people his age, he has a tendency to forget where he left his glasses, but when I ask him the scientific name of a moth he collected when he was seven, he comes up with it immediately, along with its common name and all of its characteristics. Even after fifteen years together, I was so amazed at some of the things I was discovering that I could hardly wait to call my editor with the details. If we hadn't done this book, some incredible facts might never have seen daylight.

Life shows no signs of slowing down. Ben is now working on a new book, revising *Baby and Child Care* for the sixth edition, writing his regular column for *Redbook*, filming his first video on child care, completing a documentary film of his life, and regularly crossing the country in his demanding speaking schedule. And, of course, continuing his work for peace, which he has always said he wants to be remembered as inseparable from his other work. We hope this book is a step in that direction.

*Mary Morgan*

*First birthday: the world was Ben's oyster.*

*Left: Hiddy and Anne, mother, Ben, and Betty: Ben has turned wistful.*

*Below: Bob, Anne, Betty, Hiddy, and Ben in New Harbor, Maine.*

*Opposite above: Half the 1924 Yale crew practicing aboard the S.S. Homeric en route to the Paris Olympics. Rowing machines were screwed into the ship's deck, and passengers watch.*

*Opposite below: Members of Joe Contini's extra gang on the Canadian Pacific Railroad going to work on a handcar.*

Above: Doctors from the Navy Base Hospital, Lion 9, en route from Long Island to California, August 1945.

Below: Mother, Mike Spock, and his bride, Judy, at their wedding, April 1955.

Opposite above: The gold watch chain proves useful while teaching first-year students in the family clinic at Western Reserve Medical School.

Opposite below: Terrible form—the back should be vertical, my whole body should be almost squatting.

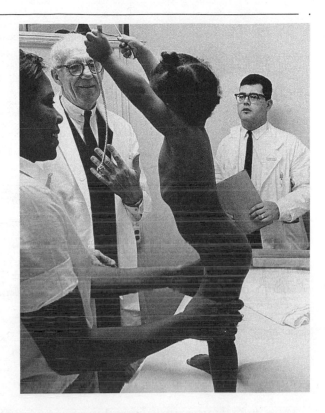

*Above: Charlie Chaplin and Ben, in scarlet gowns, receive honorary degrees at Durham University, England, 1962.*

*Below: First civil disobedience, at the Whitehall Street Induction Center, New York City, December 5, 1967.*

*Above: Being booked in The Tombs, New York City, December 5, 1967.*

*Below: Marching with Martin Luther King, Jr., against the war in Vietnam, Chicago, 1967.*

*Left: Mary and Ben emerge
from the sea in the British
Virgin Islands.*

*Below: Ginger and Ben,
reconciled, Stockton,
California, January 1985.*

# SPOCK ON SPOCK

*Ben at 3 months with his mother.*

# I

M̲Y̲ ̲M̲O̲T̲H̲E̲R̲ had all of her babies at home in New Haven, Connecticut. She wouldn't think of going to a hospital. She made the obstetrician set up a delivery room in a bedroom of our house. For a while she had a baby every two years (the sign was always the same: her craving for guava jelly). It was very exciting for us children, and the whole house was turned upside down. There was not only the delivery with all its mystery but also a trained nurse who would come and stay for a couple of weeks. From a child's point of view this was a big invasion. Not a hostile invasion; it just threw all the established balances off.

Though my mother was a puritan about sex, I don't think of her as being squeamish about birth. The fact that the doctor came and delivered a baby at home at intervals throughout my childhood gave me a realistic view of where babies come from. When I was thirteen or fourteen, she gave me a serious talk on the father's role; my father was too shy to tell me about it.

When I think about my family, I first have to remember the child who was born dead before me. His name was William, after my paternal grandfather. We hardly ever mentioned William in

*Sally Spock.*

the family, and I repeated this silence when the first baby Jane and I had was born prematurely and died. So I was the first live baby. Marjorie came a year later. (She was always known as Hiddy—that was the nearest I could get to "Sister," which Mother tried to teach me when I was one and a half.) Betty was born when I was three, Anne when I was five. Bob came more than four years after Anne, when I was nine. I was thirteen when Sally was born.

When Hiddy was just able to sit up—she was about nine months and I was two—we were in the tub taking a bath. My mother went into the next room to get something, Hiddy slipped under the water, and when Mother came back, maybe ten seconds later, she cried out, "Benny, why didn't you tell me that Hiddy was under the water?" I said, very, very slowly, as was my manner, "I was calling and calling you." My delaying might be interpreted as sibling rivalry, but I was by temperament slow in reaction time and speech. (At about three years I solemnly and laboriously told anyone who would listen, "My anitials . . . are Bee . . . Muck Ell . . . Ess." Patty Foote, Mother's best friend and sharpest rival, raised the question of feeble-mindedness.)

Mother was always concerned with health. She sometimes made her own diagnosis first, and then asked Dr. Steel, our pediatrician, to agree with her. She had read that pallor, fatigue, and whining can be symptoms of mild malaria, but Dr. Steel, our pediatrician, pooh-poohed her suggestion that there could still be malaria in New Haven. So Mother took us all to a laboratory herself, and they reported that we all had malaria. Mother bought a big book on malaria, which she later presented to me in medical school. Once she thought Hiddy had scarlet fever, which Dr. Steel denied, but when Hiddy peeled, this confirmed Mother's diagnosis. I know how irritating it is to have patients or parents make unlikely diagnoses which turn out to be right.

By the time Bob came along, I had changed a lot of diapers and given a lot of bottles. Since I was nine years older than Bob, I related to him more as a parent than as a brother. I was really Bob's regular sitter. I'd change his diapers, give him bottles, and rock him to sleep in the baby carriage on the long porch of the summer cottage in Vinalhaven, Maine. That summer's experience identifying with Mother in her love of babies was no doubt the main influence in my decision, a dozen years later, to go into pediatrics.

I felt very responsible for Bob. I would leap up from the dining table to find out why he was crying. Once I found poor Bob, at the age of nine months, hanging on to the edge of a high bureau! In his struggles to stand up in the baby carriage he slept in, he had pushed it away and was left hanging from the bureau in midair.

Bob was a serious child. He had a badly crossed eye that made him self-conscious. He had an operation to correct it, but it was only partly successful.

It was certainly a child-centered family. I think it was a reflection of this that three of the six children became schoolteachers for part of their lives and two went into child psychology. Neither parent went on vacation away from the children except on a few rare occasions when there was a compelling reason. My parents went out to a dinner party perhaps once a year at the most and gave a dinner party once every two or three years. I remember the excitement: Miss Higgins the hairdresser coming to the house and the smell of burning alcohol in her curler heater, the extra maid in the kitchen, a piece of strangely cut bread on each napkin but no butter or butter plates (no butter at dinner parties, my mother explained).

IT WAS in summer that we children were thrown most closely together because in the small, simple villages in Maine that our parents chose there were few summer children, and it never occurred to us to seek out and try to make friends with the local lobstermen's children, who seemed as strange to us as if they—or we—were foreigners. (Mother said they looked so pale because they lived on baked beans.)

As the oldest, I took the lead in initiating activities, and those who were old enough joined in. Our favorite play was with miniature sailboats, tugboats, barges, and docks, carved out of shingles and other scraps of wood, that we maneuvered in pools of rainwater on top of the granite cliffs. In the clearings in the woods we built tiny houses out of shingles, surrounding them with fences and providing them with outlying well houses that had spools and threads for hoisting pretend buckets of water from the wells. We also explored the easiest passages through the woods, where there were the least thickets, to see where they came out on the road or on the cliffs. They weren't real paths.

There was lots of minor bickering among us. I felt that my siblings were excused from blame because they were younger. My mother's typical reproach if I got in a quarrel with any of them was "Benny, you are the oldest; you should know better." All of us watched each other's table manners, and when we saw that they were lacking in any way we would call Mother's attention to them, hoping to get the offender scolded. We focused on table manners because Mother was critical in this matter. And if one of my sisters asked me to pass the sugar, I'd shorten my reach to pretend that she was closer to it than I.

We children always had an early supper in New Haven at a small children's table, which was much lower than my knees by the time I was eleven and still sitting at it. Supper would typically be cereal and applesauce. It was served always at 5:30 P.M. Most other children had dinner with their parents. But even those who had their supper separately went out and played afterward. Our mother made us stay in. We had to have our baths and be in bed and quiet by 6:45 P.M. because seven was the time my mother and father would be downstairs starting their candlelit dinner served by the Irish maid.

They allowed me to join them at this dignified ceremony when I was twelve, the same age at which my sisters and Bob would eventually join the family table. It was quite a jump from cereal and applesauce to meat and potatoes and a vegetable and then dessert. And always salad: a slice of canned pineapple on a leaf of lettuce, and a little ball of cream cheese with mayonnaise on top. I must say, I still enjoy this salad, though it's not at all a gourmet dish.

We usually had a maid, as most professional families did then in New Haven. Many of them were fresh from Ireland. My mother ruled them with an iron hand. She fired one for boiling her stockings in a saucepan, another one for lingering on the back porch to say goodnight to her boyfriend. They had to be down, of course, in time to start the long-cooking cereal for seven o'clock breakfast, and they didn't get through until they'd cleaned up after my par-

*Mother and Bob at 8 months.*

ents' dinner, which began at 7:00 P.M. They had to pull all the
shades and light the gas lamps with a taper at twilight and raise
the shades before breakfast. I think they were paid five dollars a
week.

When you're a young child, you just assume that the way your
family lives is the normal way to live: those who live less affluently
are poor, and those who are more wealthy are rich. We were
average for the neighborhood, which consisted of Yale faculty families, professionals, and junior executives in the same financial situation as my father. His salary during the middle years of my

childhood as an attorney for the New York, New Haven, and Hartford Railroad was ten thousand dollars (which, of course, bought many times what it would buy now). He was eventually raising six children and sending them to college. We got ten cents allowance per week, and we were expected to put that in the box at Sunday school, so it didn't do us much good except with the Lord. Growing up, and even when I was at college, I had to earn the money for luxuries, pleasures, and for Christmas and birthday presents for the family. I would get twenty-five cents for mowing the lawn or for raking the leaves in my early teens. When I painted my father's car, I got five dollars, which seemed like big money.

My father was referred to as a self-made man, which meant in his case that he'd had to earn his way through college and law school at Yale. He always made the point to us children that he'd had to get along without most things. But one day he let slip to us that he'd owned a sharpie sailboat, a small day-sailer with two masts and triangular sails. We immediately questioned him: "We thought you were so poor that you couldn't have anything." He was a little bit flustered and failed, as I remember, to clear up the discrepancy.


M Y MOTHER had me tonsillectomized three times. The procedure was often performed in those days for sore throats, mouth breathing, frequent colds, poor appetite, underweight. My mother took to it with enthusiasm. I was first tonsillectomized at the age of seven, at the same time as Hiddy and Betty. My mother, who dreaded hospitals, persuaded the nose-and-throat surgeon to come out to our house with his surgical team and set up in the front bedroom. Not only was I scared of the operation, it seemed very strange and frightening to have the house invaded by a surgeon, an assistant, an anesthetist, and at least a couple of nurses, so I hid behind the bedroom door until they found me.

When I was perhaps twelve, my mother and the nose-and-throat surgeon decided that I needed another operation. Of course, the tonsils hadn't really grown back, but when tonsils are removed, small buds of lymphoid tissue appear in the tonsillar space at the sides of the throat. Then they decided that I needed one more tonsillectomy when I was twenty and in college. If my mother and the nose-and-throat surgeon said that I should be tonsillectomized, on what basis could I say no?

Mother was not strongly religious in the sense of being a church-goer, though the first three children were baptized in the Episcopal Church, with godparents. All through childhood we children attended Center Church (Congregational) Sunday School because neighbors and friends went there.

On Easter Sunday there would be a ceremony at Sunday school in which the really young children came in a procession into the assembly room, each one carrying an electric candle, which gave a rosy glow to those intensely solemn faces that young children wear for ceremonies. My mother's face would turn crimson at the sight, and tears would stream down her face. All the Spock children would know that she was moved by the trusting faces of little children and that if we looked at her we would start weeping too. But we couldn't help looking.

By the time I was in Yale College, Mother insisted on taking my sisters to Yale's Battell Chapel on Sundays, to their great despair. She felt that it would be inspiring to Yale men to see such wholesome girls as her daughters in the balcony. Of course, my sisters did not want to be presented as examples of wholesomeness to Yale men, but there was no denying my mother.

Though Mother was stern with us much of the time, she always felt an obligation to be cordial to outsiders—children as well as adults. She would charm them with her storytelling and convulse them with her mimicry. Once when I was in my late teens, a neighbor, Harriett Adams, stopped by and Mother was at her wittiest. Afterward, as Harriett left, she said, "Oh, you're so lucky to have such a charming, delightful, amusing mother!" It was hard for me to think of her mainly in these terms or to answer Harriett.

But Mother's various unconventional views caused us some embarrassment, especially when she insisted that we be peculiar too.

We had to wear our winter underclothes at least a month further into the spring than other children, for fear we'd catch cold. And we were never allowed to wear sneakers as all of our friends did, because Mother believed that sneakers didn't support the ankles well enough and would be harmful to our feet.

Under great protest, three of my sisters had to wear gray angora bonnets that fit snug down to the neck and then spread out over the shoulders. My sisters looked very cute in them, I'm sure, but as no other girl was wearing anything like them, they despised them. Yet Mother insisted that they wear them when she thought it was cold enough. Once while she was walking along Cold Spring Street with her three daughters, she thought she would try to counteract their objections: she crossed the street and, pretending to be a stranger, said in a loud voice, "Oh, look at those three darling girls with their gray angora bonnets!"

M Y PARENTS were both living in New Haven when they first met. In those days, as my mother explained, there was no dating in today's sense. If a man was attracted to a young woman, he asked her if he could come to call. She would say, "Yes, come on Sunday afternoon." As long as both remained interested, he would keep coming to call, always asking permission, and after half a year or more he might then ask, "Miss Stoughton, may I call you Mildred?" She said this was an exciting stage of romance that we missed with our informality. Of course, I thought this was non-sense. In my day young people were introduced to each other as "Mister" and "Miss" but within a day or so were calling each other by first names. Nowadays they start by knowing only first names and learn the last name later, if especially interested.

When my father was courting my mother, my maternal grand-mother was upset because she didn't think he was good enough for my mother, and sent to Boston for her brother Will to come down and shoo Father away. But when Uncle Will met him, my mother said, he took a liking to him and told my grandmother that she was mistaken to object. Even without Uncle Will's backing, I doubt that my mother would have given in to her mother. She was quite determined and always sure of her devotion to Father.

My father's name was Benjamin Ives Spock. His family lived in a modest house in downtown New Haven. My grandfather had tried, when my father was a child, to get into building horse-drawn carriages but failed at this. (New Haven was as famous for carriages as Detroit is for cars.) The only remaining trace of my grandfather's carriage factory is a sled that the factory made around 1880 for my father. Painted diagonally across the top, in very fancy letters, was "Bennie." My father passed it on to me. It was a primitive type known as a "pig-sticker"—it was short, and it had a solid top and two rigid sides with wrought-iron runners. You steered it by slipping your hands into some finger spaces on the side panels and jerking it to the right or left.

My father's sister Jesamyn was married to Dr. Charlie Vishno, who, when asked how he was, would always chirp, "Able to sit up and take nourishment." Mother mimicked him exactly. My paternal grandmother lived with the Vishnos. She was a frail woman, always dressed in black lace, like my other grandmother. That's the way grandmothers were in those days.

My mother's maiden name was Mildred Louise Stoughton. Her father, Charles Stoughton, was a young colonel of Vermont volunteers in the Union Army during the Civil War. My maternal grandmother, called Nanny by us, came from a dignified Boston family named Hooper. But she was the poor end of the family because her husband, Charles Stoughton, who was dashing and handsome and wore a black patch over one eye like the Hathaway Shirt man, was not a reliable provider. In fact, he deserted her and the six children for long periods and was a womanizer. Still, my mother said, his wife continued to adore him. It is hard for me to fit that one together, because Nanny seemed quite severe to me. But my mother also told us that when she and her brother, Bradley, went up to Vermont to see their father as he was dying in an old-soldiers' home, her mother and three surviving sisters refused to go. I assume that her father's waywardness must have had much to do with my mother's fear of sex except to produce children within marriage, and with her diligence in warning us against "touching yourself down there." Once she and her father, she told me, went to an amusement park at Savan Rock, outside New Haven, and he flirted with a young woman. This incident apparently alarmed my mother a great deal.

I remember my grandmother Nanny very well because she didn't die until I was a teenager. She was a thin, haughty, stiffly erect woman in a black lace dress who seemed very severe to me. She always called me by my middle name, McLane. Nobody else in my life ever called me that.

When I was a child, Nanny lived in one of the big Victorian houses on Prospect Street. By then she had inherited money from one of her brothers. She always had a cook and a waitress/chambermaid. She always used blood oranges and red bananas, which I thought were very grand. My mother and her sisters Laura and Leila would have tea at Nanny's every afternoon, and so would

*Mildred Stoughton (second from the left) with her siblings, friends, and her mother (second from the right), about 1892.*

Bradley while he lived in New Haven after his first wife died. My mother would push a baby carriage with the youngest Spock baby, leading a parade of her other preschool children up the steep Canner Street hill. It was a very formal tea. The adults would make conversation in the parlor. The teacups were so thin that you could see sunlight through them.

We children played outside because Nanny wouldn't tolerate the boisterousness of the children. We would be invited in one by one. She would ask if we would like a cookie, and we would say, "Yes, Nanny," and she would hold out a cookie on a dish. We would advance and take the cookie and say, "Thank you, Nanny," and then go back outdoors to play. She was awe-inspiring.

WHENEVER I'M ASKED what kind of man my father was, the words that come to mind are "grave but just." I was in awe of him, but I knew I could trust him to be fair and calm in any case of disapproval. (This was in contrast to Mother, whose moral indignation colored her judgment.) Father never lost his temper or his reasonableness, though he never interfered in Mother's discipline.

My father went out of his way to be companionable with me. Before I could read to myself, he read to me *Ten Boys from History* and *The Man Without a Country*. He welcomed me when he was working on projects or repairs in the cellar. Twice he took me on trips to investigate prospective summer cottages in Maine, and once to New York to hear the opera *Madama Butterfly*, which he loved. He called me "Benno" to indicate friendliness. Yet I still think of him simply as grave but just.

When my sisters are asked what Father was like, they melt with affection and enthusiasm: "He was a darling! He called us by pet names. He told us little stories. He held our hands." Obviously, parents appear quite different to different children, but particularly to children of different sexes. In general mothers seem—and often

*Benjamin Ives Spock, counsel for the New York, New Haven and*
*Hartford Railroad.*

are—more critical of their daughters, as fathers seem to their sons,
though there are plenty of exceptions.

When my sons as adults gently reproached me for not having
shown them physical affection in childhood, I was surprised—I
explained lamely that my father had never hugged or kissed me.
I didn't remember any of my friends in our WASP neighborhood
being kissed by their fathers either. My sisters were kissed by
Father and I was kissed by Mother, but it was done briefly and
with restraint. Certainly, when we were babies we were hugged

enthusiastically. I never saw any emotional hugging, kissing, or caressing between my parents; my father would give my mother a dutiful kiss in the morning on going to work. I realize now that I assumed that intense physical affection was strictly a private part of marriage.

Three times in adolescence I felt I let my father down. When he went away on business trips, he solemnly left me in charge of the coal furnace; twice I let it go out and once was unable to get it going again before he came home. He discovered it dead and cold. He didn't scold or reproach; he just looked at me sadly, and I felt terrible. Another time, I borrowed the family car for the evening after a big football game, parked it in front of Longley's Restaurant, and forgot to lock it. When I came out, it was gone. I felt sick. I notified the police and went home to bed. When Father came in the next morning to wake me, I confessed, and again I interpreted his expression as disappointed. (Fortunately, the police found the car next morning with nothing amiss except an empty gas tank.)

When I began psychoanalysis with Dr. Bertram Lewin at the age of thirty, I complained endlessly about my mother's criticalness and domination for several months. Dr. Lewin urged me to remember my dreams, and I discovered that my mother hardly appeared in them at all—the ogres and lions and kidnappers led by association to my father and other father-figures. This is in accord with Freud's observation that the most basic rivalry—and most subtle fear—is what the son feels toward his father, mainly in his unconscious mind. So although my mother's criticalness and warnings contributed much, I think, to making me a timid child, my deeper instincts made me fear my father's anger more, even though I never saw it come out. (I ran into the same pattern in pediatric practice: when a father plays little part in discipline and completely suppresses his irritation, the son may fear the father's anger that he never sees more than another boy fears his father's ordinary disapproval and irritation.)

By the time I was a teenager I was sharply aware that my father had found his four years at Yale College extremely meaningful and rewarding. He was a member of the glee club. He was elected to DKE, a so-called junior fraternity. He was tapped for the senior society Wolf's Head. His best friend at Yale was Guy McLane, a wealthy and elegant young man from New York, who became my godfather and the source of my middle name. The fact that DKE and Wolf's Head had meant so much to my father helps to explain why I was so eager to become a regular guy and a social success at Yale. Unconsciously I must have wanted to compete with my father and to overcome my feeling throughout childhood of being a somewhat timid "mother's boy," unable to stand up to tough boys.

IN 1931, when I was an intern at Presbyterian Hospital, my father died. He was fifty-eight and died suddenly, within a few hours of a massive coronary infarction, while he and my mother were on vacation in Bermuda. They loved Bermuda. Jane and I were in the south of France. Our first baby had just died, and I had recently developed and recovered from spontaneous pneumothorax. Mother urged that we not try to come back for the funeral, and we didn't.

Despite my awe of my father and my feeling of distance from him, I know he was the one who inspired by example and built in me the obligation to be fair and reasonable, to be dependable, to be self-controlled (even though it was often carried too far), and to be dignified.

But my mother was certainly the person who most influenced my life and my attitudes. Some writers of profiles about me have implied that I got into pediatrics and wrote a book to rebel against her. To be sure, it was easy for me to conclude that there must be easier, pleasanter ways to bring up children than my mother's. But what is more fundamental and positive, I identified with her in her love of children. And her influence clearly lingered. Though

I became somewhat skeptical, for instance, about her emphasis on early bedtime and on fresh air, I found them difficult to shake entirely, and they turn up in *Baby and Child Care*.

Photographs of her as a young woman show that she was beautiful and slender with a self-confident expression. As she grew older and had six children, she put on some weight and her eyes became more intense. She retained her summer tan all winter, a color very much like that of a Native American. The clothes she bought were few and of high quality—Tailored Woman, and Frank Brothers shoes—but then she wore them when she gardened. She read a lot of novels, preferring "wholesome" stories located in English gardens. About once a year she sat down at the piano and played *Humoresque*. She was a sharp bridge player (never for money) but gave up the game when I was born, for fear she might neglect her children, and didn't resume playing (and winning) until her youngest was in college. Some of her friends had nursemaids to care for their children, but she wouldn't indulge herself in this way. She saw it as her duty to raise her children by herself.

Throughout childhood, especially in adolescence, I felt that Mother was too controlling, too strict, too moralistic. Though I never doubted her love, I was intimidated by her.

She controlled her children with a firm hand and complete self-assurance—no hesitation, no permissiveness. She never doubted that she was right in any judgment and never softened a punishment, no matter how piteously the child pleaded. She almost never used physical punishment but relied on deprivation and severe moral disapproval. When she condemned an act, her scorn could be withering. "Despicable" was an adjective she spoke with the vehemence that Jove put into his thunderbolts. But she seldom needed to depend even on scorn, because her orders and warnings were strict and unmistakable. We all grew up with consciences that were more severe than was necessary or wise. All my life, up to this day, I've felt guilty until proved innocent.

My mother died in 1968, at the age of ninety-one, after a series of strokes. In the last years of her life, her explosive resentment

*Mildred Stoughton, age 16, in 1892.*

against being an invalid under the control of others in a nursing home, instead of being in charge in her own way in her own home, had given way to a benign resignation. She no longer criticized her children or complained to the staff. Occasionally she would comment wistfully to me, "Benny, this is a strange, strange life."

*Mildred Stoughton, shortly before her marriage.*

I get my optimism, perhaps my most useful quality, from all the love and good food I received in my first year (many psychologists agree on this connection). From my mother's fierce independence of thought, her scorn for following the crowd, I surely got my independence in making up my own mind that enabled me to pioneer in the psychological aspects of pediatric practice, to see the desperate need for disarmament, to condemn Lyndon Johnson's escalation of the war in Vietnam. It was her idealism that inspired the same perspective in all her children.

*The Spock family home at 165 Cold Spring Street, with its sleeping porch where the Spock children slept summer and winter.*

# 2

IN NEW HAVEN the corner we lived on, Cold Spring Street at Everit Street, was a particularly child-infested spot. The Spocks, with eventually six children, were at the corner. To our right lived the Jacksons with their seven kids, and behind us on Everit Street in a big, grand house the Bennetts had six or seven. So there were twenty children in three adjoining houses. President Hadley of Yale referred to it as Offspring Street.

Our backyard had three cherry trees and two pear trees and lots of play equipment put there very deliberately by my mother: a merry-go-round that was more like a circulating seesaw, a sandbox that got a fresh load of clean, white sand every spring, a swing that seated three and hung from four ropes. So we played some of the time in the backyard, but we were free to ride our bikes around and go over to somebody's house without permission, or go to Mill River to search for polliwogs.

Before I started school, Mansfield Horner was my most regular companion because he was my age and lived only a short block away. Mansfield was a self-assured, joking kind of a boy, while I was timid. As we were getting toward adolescence, whenever we saw a couple snuggling in a car Mansfield would yell, "Spooning!" I thought this was terribly fresh and risqué of him.

Mansfield had Lionel electric trains of the standard size, much bigger than the ones people buy now—the cars were as big as shoe boxes. I was dying for one, but my parents never gave me playthings as expensive as that, and I wouldn't have dared ask for a toy train.

I would often be invited to Mansfield's house to play and to stay for supper. My mother, always occupied with a baby at bedtime, read to us occasionally, but his mother read aloud quite regularly. My favorite story was "The Cozy Lion," about the children of a town who discover and befriend a lion out in the woods; the adults are scared to death. The idea of children having more bravery, resourcefulness, and power than adults appealed to me tremendously.

In 1918, when I was fifteen years old, American troops came home from Europe after World War I and marched in a tremendous parade on Fifth Avenue in New York. The Horners invited me to drive down to New York with them. The parade lasted hours and hours. It was a steady, undulating column of marching soldiers in khaki uniforms, with bands playing and flags flying, as far as you could see. People were cheering and greeting them with great respect. They were felt to be heroes who had fought a brave and just war. When World War II ended, there was nothing as ceremonial as that, no parades that I remember—soldiers, sailors, and airmen were just hustled in and out of personnel depots somewhere.

ANOTHER FRIEND WAS Chunky Robbins. He was a rather bossy, slightly fat boy, very cheerful and friendly. When I was eleven years of age I was playing in Chunky's backyard one morning with five or six other boys. Chunky went into the house for some reason or other and came out holding a big bunch of bananas and proclaimed, "Everybody's gotta eat a banana!" Well, my mother, who followed exactly the health precepts laid down by Henry Holt in *The Care and Feeding of Children*, had been led to believe that bananas were a dangerous food for young children. She said that we couldn't even taste a banana until we were twelve, and then we could only eat half a banana. So I was confronted with a serious crisis, but it only took me a few seconds to realize I was much more scared of my mother than of Chunky Robbins, so I said in a timid voice, "My mother says I can't have half a banana until I'm twelve."

A year later, when I first had permission to eat half a banana, I was rather apprehensive, imagining that if I was more sensitive than the average child it still might kill me.

Another food that Dr. Holt vigorously condemned was cucumbers. Once when I was on a small excursion steamer on the Damariscotta River, I saw a boy about my age (ten) sitting at the stern and munching a whole cucumber. I watched, absolutely horrified, expecting him to keel over dead.

Chunky's sister, Adelaide, who was perhaps four years older, went to the same Sunday school as I did, and was in the Christmas play. Every year the Christmas play was the same. The setting was the stable in Bethlehem, the cock crows, "Christus natus est!" and the bull bellows, "Ubi?" and the sheep bleats, "Baaaaaaathlehem." There were parts for several shepherds and angels, and for Mary, Joseph, and the Wise Men. One year I was designated to be Joseph when Adelaide Robbins was the Virgin Mary. I felt that I was compromising her by being on the stage as her husband, as if I were intruding sexually into her life.

Next door to the Horners lived the Sargent twins, Bill and Tom. Tom seemed aggressive to me. He had a friend Babe Hopkins, and they would occasionally appear in our backyard, threatening the younger kids. I certainly didn't like bullies at all.

Bill Sanford lived way downtown. I was invited to visit him every summer for a couple of weeks at Weekapaug, Rhode Island, where his family had a cottage. It was great to come to where the water was reasonably warm, since it was too cold for swimming in Maine.

Dr. and Mrs. Sanford wanted to foster friendship between Bill and me because he was considered a nervous child and I was on the lethargic side.

Dr. Sanford was a surgeon and the physician for the Yale football team. He was also a naturalist who collected rare bird skins. He kept these unstuffed skins in cold storage. I thought that that wasn't much of a collection when nobody could see it. Later I realized that showing off the skins was not the most important thing; it was having them. He once took Bill and me down on the train to the Bronx Zoo when we were eight or ten years old. What I remember most about that trip was seeing an Italian woman nursing her baby. I was astonished that a woman would show her breasts in public.

Another time we had lunch on the battleship *Utah*. Dr. Sanford must have known somebody in the Navy who arranged this. We went to the shoreline of Manhattan and boarded a very fancy admiral's-barge; the sailors saluted. It took us to the Brooklyn Navy Yard, where the *Utah* was in drydock, but the crew and the officers were still living aboard. We had our lunch in the officers' mess, a very splendid room. What impressed me most was the silver service on a sideboard: teapots, creamers, sugar bowls, huge silver trays, coffeepots, and vegetable dishes, all of sparkling silver. I had no idea that life for officers was so elegant.

Dr. Sanford also collected moths, an interest which he fostered in me. Up till then I'd only known about clothes moths, not the large, night-flying moths that are as beautiful as the most beautiful butterflies and have caterpillars the size of a sausage or a frank-furter. We'd go on caterpillar hunts in Weekapaug with Dr. San-ford, looking up at trees. Most species of caterpillar will eat the leaves of only one tree or bush, and Dr. Sanford knew which trees to scrutinize very carefully. Tomato moth caterpillars, with their bright, poison-green color, you'd find in a tomato bed. We'd collect the caterpillars and feed them the kind of leaves we had found them on, until they went into the chrysalis stage. They'd shorten up, bulge, burst their last skin as caterpillars, and become chrys-alises. Then you'd save the chrysalis all winter, preferably in rotten wood that you'd baked in the oven to kill all the parasites that otherwise would eat the chrysalis. In the spring the moths would hatch out in perfect condition, ready for mounting.

The Sanfords also had a large petunia bed beside the cottage in Weekapaug, planted specifically to attract moths at dusk. We'd be out in the petunia bed with nets, and suddenly moths the size of hummingbirds would fly in with wings beating so fast you couldn't see them, and they'd hover over the petunias to suck out the nectar. You'd position your net just down below and swoop up, because when startled they would tend to fly slightly downward. Then you'd rush into the house and in the light see which kind of moth you'd caught. I still remember some of the names: *Cytheronia regalis*, rare, beautiful, reddish-brown and yellow in color. There were at least twenty varieties of sphinx moth. They were unusually speedy, shaped like a pursuit plane with sharp, pointed wings.

I WAS ANXIOUS as a young child in all respects, and particularly scared of lions. The whole block next to us in New Haven was a vacant lot: not a forest but a thicket of bushes of various sizes. It looked like a jungle to me, and I knew that lions live in jungles, so I assumed that there were lions there.

I'm not sure just why, but I was also scared of Italians. Wherever a ditch or the foundation of a house was being dug, Italians did the manual labor. In spring Italian women would come down the street, three or four together, dressed in peasant clothes, bandan- nas around their heads and voluminous skirts, and either holding a huge bag or wearing a folded apron around their waists. They would walk onto people's lawns and dig up the dandelions and drop them into their bag or apron. I was terrified of these women. Once when I saw one half a block away, I rushed into my house, slammed the vestibule door, and peered out the window with my heart palpitating. I imagine somebody had told me that they kidnap children and put them in those great big bags; or maybe I wasn't told that but it was all tied up with birth fantasies.

I was *very* scared of going out at Halloween. I knew that other kids would be doing naughty things like turning over trashcans or sticking pins in doorbells to keep them ringing. I was afraid that if I went out with kids who were doing these things, the householder might get very angry or even call the police. Or maybe even the police might be lurking here and there, arresting naughty boys.

I was susceptible to teasing. I certainly never teased other children or made up stories as a joke. When I was around five, Mansfield Horner took me to the head of the cellar stairs in his house, opened the door, and pointed down into the darkness, saying there was a dinosaur living under those stairs. I was somewhat skeptical, but I must have thought it was possible because I remember trying to make out the dinosaur in the dark.

Mansfield eventually became president of Pratt and Whitney, the airplane engine manufacturer in East Hartford. In adulthood I met a young engineer who worked there and told him about the dinosaur. He laughed and said, "He's just the same now."

*Benny, age 7.*

*Feeding Mrs. Judge's chickens in Brooklin, Maine, 1904.*

# 3

WHEN I WAS A YEAR OLD, I developed "summer complaint," a term that was used for severe diarrhea in infancy. Babies used to die by the thousands every summer before the care of milk had been perfected. It was milk contamination that caused summer complaint, but people didn't know that then. Anyway, my parents were despairing and somebody suggested that they take me to Maine. They did, and just as soon as I felt the cold air of Maine, the pink came back into my cheeks and I stopped having diarrhea. We stayed at Mrs. Judge's Boarding House, a farm in Brooklin, Maine.

For a number of summers after that we didn't go back to Maine but stayed at various places on Long Island Sound. When I was seven, we rented a cottage on Cushing Island, in Portland Harbor. Half of the island was a polite summer resort, and the other half was a coast artillery fort. That summer I had my first dark-blue wool suit, which has been a trademark of mine ever since. It made me feel grown-up and rather grand. It had a so-called Norfolk jacket; there was a pleat down both sides of the front and down both sides of the back, and a belt went through the pleats. I didn't wear a shirt with it, but there was a starched Buster Brown collar that buttoned into it which, instead of standing up straight, spread out. It was the kind worn by Buster Brown, the favorite comic book character in those days, who was always up to naughty adventures with his dog, Tigue.

The trip to Maine was the big event of the year. We always went by train from New Haven to Boston. My father, being an official of the railroad, always had a stateroom for us on the trip. When I was a small child, I remember with delight my father bringing along miniature trains made out of some kind of light metal. The cars were about an inch and a quarter long, and I would make them run up and down the windowsill all the way from New Haven to Boston.

In New Haven we'd go to the railroad station in a horse-drawn carriage with two horses. The upholstery was of a green color that had started as black, and it smelled of mildew; I remember how the drivers were beery-smelling. When we got to Boston we would go by another horse-drawn carriage over to the Eastern Steamship docks. There was an overnight ship to Portland, another one to Bath, another to Rockland. Then next morning we'd transfer to a small local steamer that would take us to our final destination.

One of the events of the layover in Boston was my father getting the hammocks transferred from South Station to the Eastern Steamship docks. In Maine we always had a relatively small cottage, without running water, for six children plus two parents (the one at Pemaquid Point had only two bedrooms), so my father always looked for a cottage with a big porch where he could sling hammocks for the children. He packed two hammocks to a crate and had to get them off the train, into a horse-drawn express wagon, and up to the docks. Father would shepherd the longshoremen who trundled these crates, along with all the trunks filled with clothes for the children and adults, cooking utensils, bedding, bath towels—a tremendous load of stuff. So it was a triumphant moment when Father arrived, wearing his boater straw hat and sweating like a horse. My father was a great perspirer.

The kids were usually left in charge of the Irish maid—a different one every year or so—who went along, while my mother took care of the baby—every other year there was another baby. Well, the maid, of course, didn't have the same ideas about child care as my mother. The water of Boston Harbor was filthy with garbage and trash of different kinds. Once the maid discovered a dead cat undulating in the water right by the steamboat, and she became so excited that she rushed to get all the children. I can still remember my mother's disapproval of the maid pointing out the dead cat. Such a morbid spectacle was not suitable for her children.

The maids, fresh from Ireland, would have no idea what the coast of Maine was like, or of how few Catholics there were in the small fishing villages where we spent the summers. Our cottage was always on granite cliffs, and the surf would be pounding all day and all night, especially loud after a storm. There was often fog. I remember one maid coming to my mother, sobbing with homesickness. "Mrs. Spock, I'm so *lonely!*" My mother, though she probably felt sympathy, would show no indecision. "Kitty," she said, "you agreed to come here to Maine, and you've got to stay. I don't want any nonsense." But she did relent enough to find one or two other Irish girls from nearby communities to go together in a horse and carriage to church in Damariscotta with the understanding that they were to come back promptly after church to cook Sunday dinner. They usually came home all cheered up.

O NE OF THE THINGS we children always dreamed of was to have supper in the dining saloon of one of those steamboats and have the white-coated black waiters serve us. (Saloon on a ship doesn't mean just drinks.) But, of course, my mother would have brought wholesome sandwiches from New Haven, and we'd sit munching them in our cabin or on the deck. Once when my father took me with him to Maine a couple of times to inspect possible summer cottages, he took me down to the dining saloon. I was excited to be there with the other passengers. But instead of something rather grown-up, my father ordered milk toast for me—very crisp toast, buttered and salted and covered in a soup bowl with scalding-hot milk. It tastes good enough, but I was chagrined that I had to eat small-child food in the adults' dining saloon. When my father ordered it, the waiter chuckled and said, "We call that graveyard stew." I don't know whether he meant that it was food for old people without any teeth or whether the shape of the toast reminded him of tombstones.

I was fascinated as much with steamers as with trains. I dreamed about them and I collected the timetables of all the Eastern Steamship line boats. These timetables had plans of the boats so that you could see what size the cabins were on the different decks and how much they cost. The most beautiful, from my point of view, were the S.S. *Belfast* and S.S. *Camden*, which plied between Boston, Rockland, and ports on the Penobscot River all the way up to Bangor, then turned around at Bangor, started back again in the late afternoon, and came into Rockland Harbor after sunset. These large white steamboats would be all lighted up, their searchlights playing on the Rockland breakwater lighthouse. In memory it is still a magnificent sight.

T HE NEXT TWO SUMMERS, 1911 and 1912, we went to Pemaquid Point. It was a small summer colony with no more than six or eight summer cottages and a small hotel: absolutely no communal life or social obligations, and everybody minding their own business, which made it ideal to my mother. The lighthouse there is said to be the most photographed lighthouse in America. We spent most of the summer playing on top of the cliffs because there were depressions in the rock and pools of water where Hiddy and Betty and I sailed miniature boats I made out of shingles. That's where my love of boats first surfaced.

Those two summers we lived in a tiny cottage that had only two bedrooms but a big wraparound porch for the children's hammocks.

(There were only four of us at that time; Bob and Sally hadn't been born.) My father would come up for at least every other weekend from New Haven because, as a lawyer for the New York, New Haven & Hartford Railroad, he had railroad and pullman passes and it didn't cost him anything. On weekends when he would be coming, my mother would walk to Minnie Martin's store to buy lobster, baked beans, and brown bread. She couldn't bear to boil the lobsters alive herself.

After two summers at Pemaquid Point we spent one summer at Vinalhaven, then the next five or six at New Harbor, about three and a half miles up the road from Pemaquid Point. But my mother still wanted Minnie Martin's lobsters, baked beans, and brown bread when my father would be coming. So it was my job then to walk from New Harbor to Pemaquid Point and carry them back— seven lonely miles altogether. It would take two or three hours. After a while I dared to go by the granite cliffs, which was really— looking back at it—a crazy thing to do, because it meant climbing up and down cliffs and leaping across chasms. If I had slipped and fallen, there would have been nobody to find me.

My mother was very particular about her children's diet, es- pecially her first child's, and baked beans were never allowed by Dr. Holt in *The Care and Feeding of Children.* My mother felt she was rash enough in giving each of us two baked beans and one small lobster claw. Years later I found that Andover, like most New England boarding schools, had a tradition of serving baked beans for Saturday night supper and Sunday morning breakfast. My first Saturday, I was delighted to see the student waiter come in with huge plates heaped with baked beans and set one down in front of me. From two baked beans to a plate of them—I couldn't believe my luck! I gobbled up the whole plateful, then asked for and got seconds. However, after a few months of that my eagerness for beans disappeared; I ate them because there was nothing else to eat, but without any particular enjoyment.

. . .

WHEN MY FATHER would come up to spend his weekends or his two-week vacation with us in Maine, my mother would engage Mr. Hanna, of the Hanna Livery Stable in New Harbor, to meet my father a dozen miles away in Damariscotta, the nearest train depot, and bring him back. The horse that Mr. Hanna usually drove or rented to us, Goff, had some form of indigestion and would give a small fart with every step when he trotted—poop, poop, poop. Though my parents were very proper, they couldn't help laughing at these explosions from Goff, so it was permissible for all the rest of us to laugh uproariously too.

We got our first car when I was eleven or twelve. Our first gasoline car was a second-hand Dodge, and later we had a second-hand Reo, made by the same company that eventually turned out the Oldsmobile. I remember the Dodge particularly, because by the time it got up to thirty miles per hour it was roaring so loud that you couldn't make your voice heard.

But before those came my mother's electric car. Like a Victoria carriage, it was designed for two people and had a Victoria hood, which starts small where it attaches in back to the car or carriage and then enlarges as it goes up, so that the front part extends well out over the seat. When you sat there, you were perched high up and were protected by leather mud guards. Instead of a steering wheel, it had a rod or tiller and one pedal, which was the brake. To the left of the driver, who sat in the left-hand seat, was a lever that made the car go forward or reverse; the farther you pushed it forward, the faster the car went. There was also, on the floor, a funny little button that rang a bell to warn people to get out of the way. Its top speed was maybe ten miles per hour. It ran with a purring noise. At night it was driven onto the lawn and plugged in to charge the batteries overnight.

My mother was one of the first women to drive a car in Maine. In 1914 relatively few people anywhere had cars, and very, very few families in Maine did. It never occurred to anybody that the mother or a daughter of a family could drive it, just the father. When people in Maine sitting on their porches or their front steps saw our Reo coming down the road driven by a white-haired woman, their jaws dropped open and they just stared.

My mother was independent as a driver, as in anything else that she did. In those days, in Maine, the roads were high-crowned dirt—the main roads would be tar, but always with a high crown. When we would come up behind a man who was driving slower than we were, my mother would honk the horn to get him to pull over. With the high-crowned road, pulling over meant he went almost into the gutter and his car tipped to one side. Instead of speeding up and passing him, though, my mother would just stay behind him. He would signal with his arm: Come and pass, I'm over on the side of the road and in an uncomfortable position. I would tell Mother, "You sent him to the side of the road, now pass him!" But she didn't want to pass him right then; she wouldn't think it was an ideal time. So pretty soon in exasperation he'd come back to the middle of the road. My mother would immediately honk at him again, and it would start all over again. I can still hear her saying, "But I don't *want* to pass now."

PROFESSOR PETRUNKEVITCH, a biologist from Yale, had a cottage near ours at Pemaquid Point. When we heard that he collected spiders, we thought we would help him. Under our cottage was a great big fat marble-weaving spider. I suggested that we kids (a couple of sisters and William Foote and I) collect this specimen for the professor, even though I was scared to death of spiders. (I still am at the age of eighty-six.) The idea was to catch the big spider in a jar. I, as the oldest, took the jar and approached inch by inch to where the spider was hanging on its web. Suddenly the spider made a move, and in fright I dropped the jar and backed away. When we cautiously approached again, there was the spider inside the jar. I got back enough courage to screw on the lid, and we rushed to the professor. He had for collecting specimens a jar as big as a coffee can, with alcohol and four inches of dead spiders in it. He tipped our jar upside down with his hand spread underneath, but instead of falling into his hand, the spider dropped onto his clothes and ran up around the back of his neck. The professor wasn't scared at all—he just groped around until he caught the fat spider. I was amazed that anyone could be that brave.

T HE SUMMER Bob Spock was nearing the age of one year and I was nine we spent on Vinalhaven Island, across the Fox Islands Thorofare from North Haven, which had many big elegant summer houses and a yacht club. Boston and New York people went there for the summer. The house we lived in and the one next door to it were owned by the Coolidges from Boston.

That summer I was invited to the oldest Coolidge girl's party, maybe for her thirteenth birthday. There must have been twenty-five boys and girls there, mostly proper Bostonians who knew each other. I felt socially insecure. When the time came, Mrs. Coolidge announced that every boy would invite two girls to march in to supper. I'd never been trained to escort girls in to a meal, but I quickly chose the birthday girl and her best friend. When they put their hands through my elbows, I instinctively yanked back, pulling my arms free. I glanced up and saw one of the girls give the other one an amused look at my uncouthness.

When I was in my seventies I referred to that episode in an article about how uncouth boys appear to girls who are beginning to be romantic around eleven, twelve, thirteen. The Coolidge birthday girl saw my piece and wrote me a friendly note that she wasn't holding my behavior against me.

This same summer Guy McLane invited my father to be his guest on a trip to Europe. My father had never been to Europe, nor had my mother. Though she was a jealous, possessive person, she must have encouraged him to accept this magnificent invitation, because if she hadn't I'm sure he wouldn't have gone. After my father left, my mother had the idea that she would like to send

*Ben marching in his father's twentieth college reunion parade, 1915.*

him individual pictures of the whole family. She hired a horse and carriage, and we drove five or ten miles to the town of Vinalhaven and had some pictures taken. They were surprisingly good, but my mother disliked intensively what she called the "smarty" or "cocky" expression on my face, as if I was very pleased with myself. That was the one thing my mother could not tolerate. She felt so strongly about this that she hired the horse and carriage again and drove me across the island. In the second photo my smarty expression was almost wiped off.

In my seventies I was one of the subjects in Erik Erikson's graduate seminar at Harvard called "The Case History." He would invite a well-known person to talk about his life history for three hours in the morning. Then, after lunch, the students would interrogate him for a couple of hours. Later the students sent me a copy of their conclusions. They pointed out, among other things, that this was the only time my father had been away for more than a few days, and by Freudian analysis this is probably why I was smarty and cocky. I was "cock of the roost."

*Too cocky, by far.*

*Reunion at Hamden Hall. Ben in the last row behind
Headmaster Cushing.*

# 4

M Y MOTHER had very positive ideas about children's education. She believed, for example, that it would be better for children to start their formal education at age seven rather than six. A great educator, Caroline Zachry, was the first to explain to me that in experiments with holding off on the formal aspect of reading, writing, and arithmetic until the age of seven, the children learned more readily and had distinctly fewer problems with reading and arithmetic.

Caroline would roll over in her grave if she could hear about today's "superkids" who are taught to read at the age of two. I believe a lot of our troubles come from the excessively competitive attitudes of our society. "Get ahead, kid—that's what you're in the world for" is the message that many children get. Conscientious parents even come to feel guilty for *not* pushing their children in this way. None of them seem to question whether there is any sense or purpose to it. My feeling is that the child is hurt—abused— by that amount of pressure and misled as to the importance of early academic learning. Children at two, three, and four years of age naturally want to spend their time learning how to get along with other children and with adults, as well as playing at being mothers and fathers. This is infinitely more valuable than reading and writing.

The summer after I turned seven without having gone to school, my mother apparently felt some kind of guilt, because she bought a primer and sat me down and sternly explained that d-o-g was "dog" and c-a-t was "cat." I was scared to death of her, and most of the times she pointed to "cat" or "dog" I got it wrong. Within ten minutes she lost the little patience she had, grabbed me by the hair, shook my head until my teeth rattled, and said, "Benny, how can you be so stupid?" She called off the rest of that lesson. The next morning she tried again. And again I was wrong more often than right, and again she shook my head. The whole tutoring campaign lasted only two days, fortunately for both of us. When parents asked me as a pediatrician whether they should tutor their child, I suggested that they first find out whether they have any patience. If a parent cares too much and gets too agitated about mistakes, it can petrify the child.

Mother approved highly of reading, and she filled the house with books like *The Book of Knowledge* and sets of Mark Twain, Thackeray, Dickens, Kingsley, and Stevenson; I remember especially *Treasure Island* and *Black Arrow*. Yet if she found me reading, she would immediately find something for me to do—clean up my room, mow the lawn, rake the leaves. So I would have to find a secret place to read.

At age seven and a half I finally started going to a school run by Bill Sanford's governess, Miss Ogden, in the Sanfords' house. I doubt that she'd had any formal instruction in teaching. The idea for the school must have come from the Sanfords and been agreed to by other parents. Hiddy and I attended, along with four other neighborhood kids. We walked the mile from our block to the Sanfords' house both ways every day.

Miss Ogden assigned work according to capability. In the second year I came to long division. Either long division is unsuitable for eight-year-olds or I was too slow or too inhibited to learn it. There were just too many complex steps. When I felt totally confounded and defeated each day by it I would cry. I don't remember Miss Ogden taking mercy on me. That's probably unfair. I was overly sensitive to people who weren't overly sensitive to me. At any rate, I couldn't have gone on crying forever: either I caught on or Miss Odgen, seeing that I was incapable of the intricacies of long division, yielded.

After two years in Miss Ogden's class, when I was nine I started in the third grade at Worthington Hooker School, a public school very close to our house. My classroom was divided into two classes: the upper third grade (mine) and the lower fourth grade. We had different work to do. The more advanced half was reading *Heidi*, which seemed much more interesting, much more dramatic than what we were reading. In art class the monitor would pass out pieces of paper to each student and, for instance, a fall-colored maple leaf. We then sat and copied the leaf in crayon. We weren't meant to be creative in any sense.

I enjoyed being at Worthington Hooker because I was a regular pupil going to a regular school in my own neighborhood. And I certainly didn't have to cry in this class. There was a girl two rows away from me who I thought was very beautiful and somewhat wistful. I watched her out of the corner of my eye a good deal.

But after two months I was taken out of Worthington Hooker. Some of the parents who were infected with the current idea that fresh air had great value (my mother was certainly one of those) got together with the idea of starting an "open-air" school. They persuaded the board of education to provide a teacher, a large wooden platform, a tent, twenty desks, and twenty thick felt bags to sit in.

Professor and Mrs. Hocking consented to play host to this school. Professor Hocking was an assistant professor of philosophy who subsequently became head of the department at Harvard. His young Irish wife was very dynamic, with sparkling eyes and great enthusiasm for whatever she was doing. They had a good-sized backyard on Orange Street—an unconventional place for a house

*The fresh air school in New Haven, 1912. Ben in the back row, fourth from the left.*

because it was fairly close to downtown New Haven. Our teacher was Miss Jocelyn, a bustling, cheery, certainly unthreatening woman of fifty or so. There were perhaps twenty children of assorted grades. At nine, I was among the oldest.

Our desks were screwed to the wooden platform, most of which was under the tent. On the outside part we did folk dancing, on the assumption that on cold days it would warm us up and keep our blood circulating. There was no heating in this tent. When the temperature dropped, we sat in felt bags that came up to our armpits. We wore overcoats and, when it really got cold, knit toboggan hats, gloves, and fleece-lined boots over our shoes.

Mrs. Hocking adopted us into her family. If she discovered that it was a child's birthday, she would whip up a huge pitcher of cocoa and buy some cookies for a birthday party. When it was my birthday, she asked me to go into her house to help prepare the cocoa and the cookies. I remember very clearly that floating on top of the cocoa, in a big white enamelware pitcher, were several drops of oil. This was probably the oil of the cocoa bean, I realize now. But at the time, being a squeamish child, I thought it was some butter that hadn't been washed out of the pitcher. The idea that it was not quite sanitary was supported by the fact that the house, being very old, was rather stuffy and smelled. Children are sensitive to things that are the least bit different from the ways of their own family. But I drank the cocoa; I felt absolutely obligated. I don't think that at home we'd ever had store-bought cookies, and it seemed rather daring to be eating them.

I had no trouble academically at the open-air school. I was a goody-goody for Miss Jocelyn, while Bob McFarland was the bad boy. His father was professor of chemistry at New Haven High School, so there were a lot of chemicals in their basement and Bob and I could put our homemade bombs together. When the Winchester Repeating Arms employees would go by, we would set off our bombs. Mrs. McFarland would fly off the handle at times (because she was Spanish, my mother said).

Bob always seemed incredibly indulged to me. On weekends when I arrived at his house at 9:00 A.M., he would just be getting up and having his breakfast. There would be a half-pint of thick cream on the table, and he could pour as much as he wanted on his cereal. In the Spock family, between us we were allowed only a half-pint of thick cream for our Sunday morning rice cereal. Only an ounce of cream at the most could go to each child, and, needless to say, we watched each other suspiciously to make sure that nobody took more than their share. My father would pretend to tip the pitcher of cream way over as if he were going to take half the pitcherful on his cereal, but then we'd all gasp and he would catch it in time. On weekdays we had "top of bottle"—thin cream—for our cereal. (This was before milk was homogenized.) Was I envious of Bob!

At the open-air school he was a thorn in Miss Jocelyn's side because he wouldn't pay attention to business and would distract the other kids. He would make faces and thumb his nose to get attention. Miss Jocelyn would finally lose her patience and shout,

"Bob McFarland, go out to the little red house!" This was a small toolshed in the Hockings' backyard. Bob McFarland would peer out at us through its single, dusty, cobwebbed window and make more faces.

In their backyard the Hockings kept a goat tethered by a rope. At recess we would surround the goat, just outside his range, and taunt him. The goat would come running as if to assault whoever was teasing him. Bob McFarland would come up behind Helen Tweedy, a beautiful blond girl, and push her into the goat's range. Then the goat would rush at her and she would scream and everybody else would scream or laugh. The goat never did any damage to Helen.

Bob had skill with tools, of which there were plenty in his basement. He started to make a violin for Hiddy, though he never finished it. He built himself a small, informal automobile out of baby carriage wheels, a wide plank, and a motorcycle engine. On its first trial run down the steep Canner Street hill, it got safely across St. Ronan Street but collided with an automobile on Whitney Avenue, smashing Bob's car to splinters and injuring Bob severely. Bob later failed to make the grade in several boarding schools and in college. He joined the merchant marine and fell to his death from a scaffolding while painting a ship in drydock. It was a tragic loss of a life that could have been productive.

The second year, the school was moved to the recess yard of the Edwards Street School, a public school in a slightly tougher district than where we all came from. And we were subjected to the ridicule of some of the tougher kids, who would shout names at us. The devastating name was "hot-air kids." I felt humiliated to be so different from the students in the other school. Sometimes they would come to their classroom windows and make faces at us.

I never got into any real fights at school. I was not the fighting type. But going home from school one day, we went past the house of a rather peculiar-looking, skinny, very pale guy about my age. I pretended I was going to chase him and punch him. He cringed and backed away. No matter how timid a child or a person is, when they sense that somebody else is even more timid, it is likely to bring out the meanness in them.

At age eleven I was sent to Hopkins Grammar School, which my uncle Bradley had attended. It was a private school that had been established in the seventeenth century, long before there were any public schools in New Haven or anywhere else in America. I went there for one year, the fifth grade.

What I most remember is how run-down Hopkins was then. Today it's a fully reputable school again, but then there were only two teachers—the headmaster and his assistant—for the very small enrollment, most of whom, I had the distinct impression, had been kicked out of high school or grade school in New Haven and had to find a school that would take them. In that small enrollment there were a lot of tough guys, and at least one or two boarding students, because at recess some of the rougher boys would go into one of the students' rooms for a blanket to toss the smaller kids in the air. I was one of the smaller kids. A circle of about eight students would hold this blanket by the edges and relax their arms so that the kid in the middle was almost touching the ground, and would then, on a signal, give a yank that sent the kid up into the air maybe ten feet. It was great sport for the guys doing the tossing but scary for the kid being tossed.

There were only two or three boys at my level. One of them was a fat boy who came to class one day with his jacket pocket full of caps for a cap pistol. He squeezed the caps between his nails, and they went off with something between a pop and a hiss. The teacher heard this pop-hissing but couldn't tell who was responsible for it. All of a sudden one cap went off and set fire to all the other caps in his pocket, and he let out a howl. A black cloud came out of his pocket, and he snatched his hand out and it was black too. This made quite an impression on us. I never did anything like that.

One day when the headmaster was teaching us Latin, he sent

me to his office for some reference material. Out in the corridor I ran into two seniors, big guys, and they said they wanted me to go out to the store nearby and buy them a pack of cigarettes. Of course, I was horrified: I couldn't go out of the building, and buying cigarettes on top of that would be a double crime. I told them I couldn't, and they said I had to. Then the two of them grabbed me by the seat of the pants and ran me up and down the corridor. My toes were just barely touching the floor, and I was in danger of falling flat on my face. I never did go to the store, because I was much more scared of the authorities than of these toughs.

To get to Hopkins, a mile and a half away, I had to walk downtown, then go through the university area. There were good sidewalks all the way, so part of the time I went by roller skates, taking a shortcut through the rotunda of Woolsey Hall. The building department of Yale University really wouldn't have approved, but there was nobody to stop me.

FROM AGES TWELVE TO SIXTEEN I went to my favorite school, Hamden Hall. It was a new private boys' school in a suburb of New Haven—quite a contrast to Hopkins Grammar. The idea of a country day school like Hamden Hall was somewhat new: it was out in the country and had athletics programs. I always walked there and back and had lunch at school. I would stay there until the end of the afternoon doing athletics.

Three teachers constituted the whole faculty at Hamden Hall because the school had only forty students then, all overprotected and proper. The headmaster and math teacher, Dr. Cushing, was a gruff fellow we called "Doc" behind his back, which we thought was pretty daring. He wasn't threatening or disagreeable in any way, just a bit pompous, always saying things like "Boys, boys, stop that foolish prattle." Mr. Twitchel, who taught history, was small, wiry, and very friendly. He had huge ears that stuck out. Mr. Babcock taught Latin and French. He was a bachelor and,

*Mr. Twitchel and Mr. Babcock, about 1915.*

like Mr. Twitchel, a kind, friendly teacher. He was handsome and had tight curly blond hair. He was always immaculately groomed and always wore a blue suit with white chalk-stripes. I thought, That's the way *I* want to look. And here I am today at eighty six, still wearing a blue suit with white chalk-stripes.

To give you an idea of how relatively simple the level of instruction was, our text for ancient history was less than an inch thick— to cover the Egyptians, the Greeks, *and* the Roman Empire. The chapter heading for the Roman period had as a decoration a reproduction of the statue of the infants Romulus and Remus sitting on the ground and reaching their mouths up to the teats of the wolf. As early teenage boys (I was fourteen at the time), we were acutely aware that this rather indelicate picture would eventually come up. And when the day came that we turned to this page, the class of five boys burst out laughing, and Mr. Twitchel turned scarlet and said, "Boys, boys."

I've used that incident in writing and in speaking about sex education: it goes on, whether or not you as a parent or teacher intend it to. It can be positive in spirit or negative, as in the case of Mr. Twitchel's blush. Looking back, it seems surprising that at that stage of adolescence our interest in sexuality would be suppressed enough to make us all break out laughing at the sight of a reproduction of a statue as familiar as the Venus de Milo or the Winged Victory.

During my early years at Hamden Hall I would have loved to go to the dancing class there, but my mother thought it was silly at that age. Most of the boys who did go to dancing class protested noisily. They had to have their athletic session cut short on that day of the week to take a shower and get neatened up in their blue serge suits with knee britches.

In those days boys wore knee britches until they shot up in adolescence, which happened to me at fifteen. I was 5'8" or 5'10" when I was mercifully switched over to long pants. My father took care of that. He also took me to his tailor, I. Kleiner's, when I grew too tall and square-shouldered to wear the ready-made suits from Jay Johnson and Company on Church Street in New Haven. Mr. Kleiner, who didn't measure more than five feet tall himself, would have trouble fitting me around the shoulders. This was one of the few matters that my father, not my mother, took charge of.

The whole four years I was at Hamden Hall, from twelve to sixteen, I loved a girl named Marta Schnielock from afar. She went to my Sunday school and always sat two rows ahead of me (because she was two years older). I would look at the back of her head and call up the image of her face. She was short and dark-haired, with a misty expression but sparkling eyes. I thought she was ravishing. Something gave me the idea that she was an orphan, though it may just have been that she lived in the same house where a boy at Hamden Hall lived with his aunt and uncle. I used to daydream that I would rescue Marta from an earthquake or fire in a Pierce-Arrow racing car that belonged to a Yale student and that I coveted. I was only moderately troubled by not knowing how to drive.

I was much too timid to approach Marta in any way until my last year at Hamden Hall, when I was sixteen, at the Christmas Frolic. This was an annual all-ages party between Christmas and New Year's at the New Haven Lawn Club. Whole families, from small children to grandparents, would attend. There was dancing, but between the dances there were games, primarily for the children. For an hour I watched Marta, wondering if I would dare ask her to dance. Then, all of a sudden, I was surprised to find myself walking across the floor toward her. When I got to her I blurted out, "Aren't you Marta?"—as if there was any doubt in my mind. She admitted with a pleasant smile that she was, and we danced. I couldn't think of a thing to say; I was in a turmoil. After a while the music stopped and I deposited her back with the people she had come with. That was the only time I ever spoke to her. I wasn't bold enough to arrange another encounter.

A T HAMDEN HALL we played two organized sports: soccer in the fall (football was considered too rough and dangerous) and baseball in the spring. Mr. Twitchel and Mr. Babcock coached both. They were good athletes and could throw and catch with grace.

I was a fair athlete. As one of the oldest boys in the school (and distinctively the tallest), I was on both the soccer team and the baseball team, but baseball was my favorite. I played first base because coaches want someone tall who can put one foot on the base and lean out and make the catch if the ball is thrown a little wild. I thought that it was a responsible position but never felt very secure about it, because I couldn't always be counted on to catch the ball. During baseball practice Mr. Babcock or Mr. Twitchel hit the ball out to a number of boys spread around the field to catch high flies. Once when I reached up for the ball, it somehow came down between my two hands and smacked me right in the nose.

DURING WORLD WAR I Mr. Babcock volunteered to drive an ambulance in France for the American Red Cross. He wrote long letters addressed to the student body which either Dr. Cushing or Mr. Twitchel read to us about what it was like on the battlefront in France. He was an inspiration to us: it was a really dangerous adventure. He sent the school French war posters that exhorted the people for instance to buy war bonds. The art in these French posters was very good. One particularly famous poster depicted a soldier in a steel helmet of the French type with an inspired, excited facial expression. He is rushing forward with his gun and bayonet held high in the air, and he is shouting, "*On les aura*"—"We'll get them."

Dr. Cushing ceremoniously hung Mr. Babcock's posters around the main study hall at Hamden Hall to remind us that it was a real war that Mr. Babcock was in. Later when America entered the war, all the older boys at Hamden Hall began collecting American war posters. We haunted the Army, Navy, and Marine Corps recruiting stations in New Haven. And when the government began selling Liberty Bonds to finance the war, we collected Liberty Bond posters also.

I had a collection of a hundred World War I posters. One poster that I particularly valued asked people to contribute their binoculars to the American Navy. Most binoculars at that time came from Germany, and the Navy couldn't get enough during the war. This was a rather dramatic poster: a naval officer stands blindfolded on a ship's bridge, and it reads, "Please contribute your eyes to the Navy." Shortly after it came out the Navy decided to withdraw it because they thought that uneducated or unwise people would conclude that Navy men were losing their eyes in combat.

Since Mr. Babcock was driving an ambulance and thus not actually in combat, I doubt it ever seriously occurred to us that he might be injured or even killed. War itself seemed both romantic and somewhat unreal to us—above all, remote.

As World War I went on, it became apparent that it did not consist of cavalry charges but was a grindingly slow massacre of young men in trenches, covered with mud. (Charlie Chaplin demonstrated the wretched conditions in *Shoulder Arms* as he feels around under the water, trying to find his bed, and pulls out his blanket.) But many people at the time really didn't want to know about that aspect of it. The great, all-day welcome-home parade on Fifth Avenue with its hundreds of thousands of cheering spectators not only celebrated the armistice but helped to coat the war with glamor.

No one in our family knew anyone who was actively participating, aside from Mr. Babcock, and none of the families we knew had sons old enough to go—so we seldom talked about it. Still, my parents felt strongly enough about everyone's making a contribution to arrange with Dr. Cushing that I should help coach some of the younger boys in batting practice—a big-brother type of coach. I also helped out Saturday mornings in the carpentry class. But sometimes I completely forgot about these obligations and would be horsing around with some of the older boys. Mr. Twitchel had to remind me, very politely, that I was supposed to be helpful now.

At Hamden Hall we had a drum-and-bugle corps as our contribution to the war effort. The armed services had taken over many universities, and Yale students were now training to be Navy officers. We were to provide marching music for the Yale Navy. Every afternoon for one school year a bugler and a drummer from the Marines came out to teach us. I played the bugle. At least with drumming you don't have to stay on key, but with bugling you have to train your lips to hit certain notes and not slur them. We drummed and we bugled every afternoon, making the air hideous with our martial music.

The great day came when we were to march with the Yale Navy

*The assembly room at Hamden Hall, with Mr. Babcock's war
posters on the wall.*

in the Memorial Day parade. We had been practicing hard most
of the school year and were proud of our accomplishment. A photographer even shot us all lined up on the New Haven green waiting
to take our place in this parade. But when our big moment had
come and gone, we were mortified to find that the Yale Navy had
quickly learned to resent our little drum-and-bugle corps. We
had marched in front of the Yale Navy for two hours around New
Haven, and since most of us were little boys, they had had to take
little mincing steps to keep time with us.

One evening when I was upstairs studying, my mother and father
called me down to them at the dinner table. They reminded me
that for the war effort we needed to save wool, and they had decided
that I could wear one of my father's cast-off suits. My heart sank.
All of my father's suits were very grave, dark-gray, and this one
had a fine line in it. But not at all a sporty line—exactly what a
banker or lawyer would wear in those days to present a dignified
exterior. While the suits then in fashion for boys fit very tight and

had four buttons on the jacket (which you were to button at the top only), this suit was very loose and had only two jacket buttons, the trousers didn't even have cuffs. In my dismay I pleaded, "Everybody will laugh at me in school!" (which they did). My mother bristled indignantly: "You ought to be ashamed of yourself, worrying what people will think of you. All you have to know is that you are *right!*"

Of course, I didn't believe her at the age of fourteen, when the opinion of my peers was of the utmost importance. But her advice comforted me fifty years later when I found myself indicted for conspiracy by the federal government for my opposition to the war in Vietnam.

*Bill Sanford (center) and Ben (right) prepare to work in the victory garden at Hamden Hall, about 1917.*

# 5

THE SUMMER when my father was coming back from Europe and my mother wanted to go down to Boston to meet him, Mary Weir, who did our mending in New Haven, came to sit with us. She was perhaps thirty years of age, short, pretty, slightly plump, and I became infatuated with her. We went walking in the Maine woods, something I have always loved to do. Every few feet there are roots to step over, so I would take hold of Mary Weir's arm and make sure that she didn't trip or fall. This was the same summer when I was photographed with a cocky expression on my face.

Another object of my affections was Bill Sanford's governess, Miss Ogden. Summers when I was between nine and twelve years of age, I was invited to visit the Sanfords in Weekapaug, Rhode Island. They had a cottage off by itself with a dock and a float on Weekapaug Pond. Salt water flowed in and out of it, but a sandy bar separated it from the ocean.

Bill Sanford had a catboat called the *White Lady*, about twelve feet long. We used to go out almost daily, and Miss Ogden always went with us. She was a slender, serious-visaged young woman, maybe thirty. She was not the least bit seductive, but she was rather good-looking. One day she invited a governess from another home nearby to go sailing with us. In those days women wore skirts right down to the floor. The other governess's skirt had come up to maybe a few inches above her ankle, and when Miss Ogden saw what I was doing, she made some kind of signal to her: Look out, this boy is ogling your ankles! Right away the other governess yanked her skirt down. I felt like a sex fiend caught in the act.

I remember wondering about sex when I was eight or ten years old. One morning when I was down in the yard between our house and the Jacksons', I looked up and Mrs. Jackson was getting dressed and I saw the hair in her armpit. The idea occurred to me that that's where babies are born. I have to laugh at this because it's such an obvious case of what Freud called upward displacement: when you're too inhibited, too scared to have thoughts about the genitals, you displace your fantasies upward.

My mother frequently warned us against masturbation. Except she would never use a frank word like "masturbation"; as she phrased it, "You mustn't touch yourself down there." We also must not have "naughty thoughts." My mother led me to believe they might cause physical malformations in my children. "Benny, you *do* want to have normal children, don't you?" As soon as Michael, my first child, was born, I went to see him in the hospital's newborn nursery, then hurried back to Jane, who was still in the delivery room, and I said happily, "He has ten fingers and ten toes." So my mother's warning clearly was still on my subconscious mind, even though by that time I'd not only graduated from medical school but had completed nearly four years of internship and residency!

Once when I was fourteen or fifteen, my mother drove me down Whitney Avenue, the main drag in the genteel part of New Haven. When I saw any young woman standing on the corner waiting for a streetcar, I would turn my head to see her face. My mother caught me doing this and said, "Benny, that's disgusting!" To her, all men who looked at girls were thinking immoral thoughts—"as if they were looking at horses," she would say.

I WAS SIXTEEN in the fall of 1919 when I outgrew Hamden Hall and went to Phillips Academy in Andover, Massachusetts, where I would stay for two years. So I was to go away from home for the first time. It was a great adventure. Some kids get homesick away from home, but not I.

I entered Andover too late to get into a dormitory, so I had to live in a rooming house for part of the first year until I could replace somebody who got thrown out of his dormitory room for smoking.

A lot of boys came to Andover for just one year because they were considered too young for college. There were also men who had just come out of the Army and wanted to go on to college but needed a little more preparation. One guy in my senior class was twenty-seven years old. Needless to say, he was welcome on the football team.

To the boys it seemed like great freedom to be there, even though I suspect it was much more protective than it is now. We had to be in our dormitories at 8:00 P.M. for room check. Some of the older men didn't take kindly to those hours; we were always hearing stories about people who waited till after room check and then piled out the window and went to the nearby city of Lawrence.

The friends I made at Andover were, in general, overprotected boys like myself—not the majority of students there but certainly an appreciable number.

In my senior year at Andover my mother and father drove up to take me and a few friends to the Andover Inn for Thanksgiving dinner. That particular year they were driving an open second-hand Packard (there were very few closed cars back then; only a few old fuddy-duddies bought sedans or limousines). I was afraid of two things: that my friends would see my parents' clothing and other luggage piled up on the back seat, and that some of my mother's hair would be loose in back and curling down over her coat collar instead of neatly caught up in a bun. The secret underneath was that my friends might look down on me because of my parents' lapses. Of course, my friends were delighted to have Thanksgiving dinner at the inn. They overlooked the "mess."

Each year at Andover I went home for two weeks of Christmas vacation and a week of spring vacation. When I came home for Christmas vacation at seventeen, I was looking forward most of all to going to the small dances that New Haven parents gave for their children at that time. You'd arrive at eight o'clock, and the party would be in the living room of the family and end at eleven or twelve; a pianist and a violinist would provide the music. Hiddy and I went to these dances together and came home together. I found these parties fun for the dancing but excessively "wholesome"—my mother's word for everything she wanted in a girl or, for that matter, in a boy. "Wholesome" meant that you were preoccupied with worthwhile things like lessons, literature, and career choices. It also meant not being seductive or too interested in the opposite sex. At Andover it was hard for me to believe my classmates' stories about dates in cities like Chicago, where they would invite a girl out for dinner at a restaurant and then go on to a nightclub. Our parties were so innocent and homebound by comparison. Many of the girls at these parties were good friends of my sisters and came from faculty families. Most of them not only didn't interest me romantically but struck me as too lacking in seductiveness.

During that particular Christmas vacation the best party was going to be at the Stoddards', who lived in a great big white Georgian house surrounded by large grounds and a wall. My mother, unfortunately, disapproved of the Stoddards. She believed that they not only drank liquor, which she saw as a fault, but also corrupted the morals of college students by serving it to them. So we were forbidden to go to that party.

Well, we went up to the Stoddards' party anyway—not dressed in party clothes and not to go into the house but to greet our friends during an intermission in the music, just to defy our mother. The next day, my mother not only found out from Aunt Patty, who'd gotten it from her son, William, that we'd done the forbidden thing but felt that we had exposed her to ridicule among her friends. She was absolutely furious and said we couldn't go to any parties for the rest of that Christmas vacation.

This was the most severe punishment that could possibly have been dealt out to me. We begged and wailed and pleaded on bended knee, but my mother never once relented in any punishment she had imposed. She never doubted that any opinion of hers was other than God's own truth. She was the supreme court. So we stayed home from all the parties, gnashing our teeth.

This was the first (and last) time that I dared to defy my mother.


IN MY FIRST YEAR at Andover I had to be tutored in geometry. So long division with Miss Ogden was only the beginning of my problems with math. But in my senior year I was elected to Cum Laude, the scholastic honor society, on the basis of my grades that year in Latin, Greek, chemistry, and physics. In those days you had to take college board examinations in every subject you took. Ninety-eight on the physics exam was my highest score by far. It was to come in handy when I found out that I could use it to get accepted into medical school.

I never played football—I was too long and skinny—so I chose soccer. The school was divided into four clubs for intramural athletics, separate from varsity sports: the Greeks, Romans, Saxons, and Gauls; I played soccer for the Greeks. In one of the crucial games, at the end of the season, our opponents came dribbling the ball down the field, and one of our fullbacks, a big, awkward guy, rushed out and gave a great kick, and the ball went right under his leg and into the goal. Though it was very uncharacteristic of me to show criticism so openly, I got very angry and shouted scornfully at him.

In the spring there was no soccer, so I went out for high-jumping.

*The Andover track team, 1921. Ben on the far left
in the middle row.*

Though I remained a very undistinguished high-jumper, I was able
to jump 5′6″, and that was enough to get me on the varsity track
squad with two other high-jumpers and to win half of a third place
in the Exeter meet. It was a cheap way to get my varsity "A" for
my sweater, but it made me feel I was on my way to becoming a
regular guy and a big man on campus.

At the beginning of my senior year I was elected to a fraternity,
Alpha Gamma Chi, or "AGX." It's unusual for a high school to

have fraternities, and I doubt that they contribute positively, but I felt like a man of the world. I bought a box of heavily embossed fraternity stationery and wrote a love letter to Peggy Ramsey at Miss Masters' School, in whose presence I had always been utterly tongue-tied.

AGX had a modest clubhouse. Originally it had been a home in Andover, but all the shades were drawn to keep its secrets hidden. We could go over to our fraternity house any time of the day until eight at night. In winter, though, it was not warm enough. I offered to tend the furnace. Having done that chore for my father's furnace, I was able to make this one work so that the house was cozy and warm, and I was much appreciated for it.

THE SUMMER AFTER my first Andover year I volunteered to be a counselor at a camp for poor boys on Long Island. There I was befriended by an older counselor, a Yale junior. I told him with quiet pride that my father had been a member of the Yale Glee Club, DKE, and Wolf's Head, which showed I was already preoccupied with meeting the Yale challenge. My friend reproached me for expecting to succeed by clinging to my father's coattails, and I felt squelched.

This Yale man told me solemnly about life in general, and particularly how at a summer community in Maine he had begun keeping company with a twenty-five-year-old nurse, who then tried to seduce him. He explained to me, as an older man of the world, that I should be prepared for such temptations. This was a real eye-opener. I had no idea girls ever hinted that they were ready to go farther than the man.

At seventeen I had never even kissed a girl—I had never had a date! The closest I'd gotten was with a friend of our family named Sandra. The summer before, Sandra and I were down on the float of her family's summer house. Being on a float by ourselves on a moonlit night made me unusually impulsive, and I gave her a kiss—

just a little peck—and said, "Did you like it?" I asked because my mother had given me the idea that any advance was apt to be unwelcome to "nice" girls except in marriage. But when I asked, she just said, "Don't be silly," which was a good answer. I considered it at least a mildly successful romantic episode.

At Andover there were no girl students at that time. But one Sunday afternoon in the spring of my senior year, several friends invited me to go calling on some girls who lived on the edge of town. Certainly I had always been interested in girls, even if I still couldn't talk to them, so I accepted.

These were girls from a respectable family in town. But as soon as I got there I realized that they were more casual, more worldly, than my sisters or their friends—they weren't at all shy. During this afternoon call one of the girls suggested that I come out to the pantry and help her prepare some cookies and some Cokes. I went, and at a certain point she said to me, "Do you know that you are very attractive?" Well, that was exciting! No girl in New Haven would have been bold enough to say such a thing to me! I had never kissed a girl and wanted to very much, but now I was petrified. While I was helping her arrange the cookies on a plate and getting out glasses and Cokes and ice cubes, I kept saying to myself, I bet I can kiss her, I bet I can kiss her, I bet I can kiss her. After about five or ten minutes the stuff was ready and we went back into the living room. When the opportunity came, I didn't take advantage of her great cordiality. In fact, I chickened out.

A few years earlier, after one of my mother's friends had complimented me on my looks, my mother had told me, "Benny, you are not attractive-looking. You just have a pleasant smile." She was scared that I would become corrupted if I thought I was good-looking. Now I foolishly wrote to her that I had gone with friends to visit some girls at their house, and I boasted that one of them had told me I was attractive. This alarmed the hell out of my mother, and immediately she wrote back, "Benny, it seems clear that you lost your ideals at Andover, and that when you come back to New Haven to go to Yale next fall, you should live at home to try to recover them." This was a terrible blow. The whole point of going to college was to live on campus and get away from my mother's supervision.

Years later, when my mother died, I found this very letter. When I read it, I realized I wasn't merely reporting an incident. I was clearly trying to taunt her—and I certainly succeeded, to my dismay.

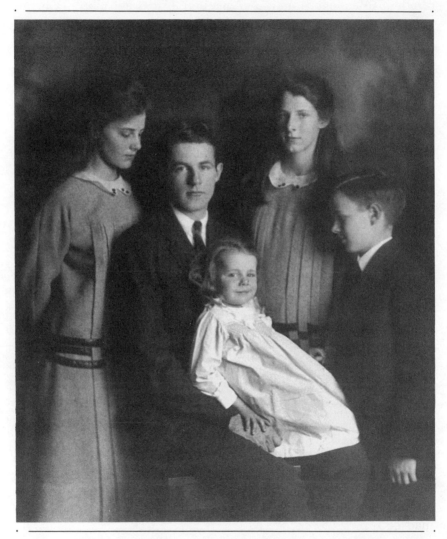

*Betty, Ben, Sally, Anne, and Bob Spock, around 1922.*

# 6

I ENTERED YALE in 1921, at the outset of the Roaring Twenties. There was meant to be license, I knew, compared to prewar times—skirts got unbelievably short, and some girls were allowed to go out of town to college proms without chaperones. Some classmates described the delights of dating. Others got drunk on Saturday night. I daydreamed about such a life, but I took it for granted that none of it was for me. I was actually timid and virginal. Come near a girl? The one time I dared go to the movies, Patty Foote showed up and later said to my mother, "Guess who I saw at the movies: Benny!"

There was never any question in my mind or in my family's mind that Yale was the college I was to go to. That's where my father had gone. In those days you went to your father's college, unless you couldn't get in. And I was inspired by my father's example to succeed at some extracurricular activity and hoped to be elected to a fraternity and a senior society.

At that time, most Yale students were more concerned with athletics, social life, and girlfriends than with their courses. You took it for granted that you had to pass them, but only the grinds tried for high grades. Clothes were important too: you wore a suit, or else slacks and a tweed jacket, a white shirt with a button-down collar, and a tie. Everybody had to wear a felt hat except seniors— as a privilege of the senior year, you could go without a hat.

In my freshman year I had to live at home at first, except that my parents allowed me to share a room during the day for studying between classes. My New Haven friend Ted Hume and his room-mate, Ting (Huntington) Sheldon, a very elegant American who had grown up in England and gone to Eton, let me share their room. I went home to have supper, to study, and to spend the night.

When I had to live at home again, I felt myself at a hopeless social disadvantage. Between classwork and living at home, I had little time to hang around with my friends and acquaintances from Andover or make new friends.

Even as a college man, my experience with women was woefully limited. Marta had been the girl I loved from the back row of Sunday school until I was sixteen, when the object of my affection became Peggy Ramsey, whom I worshiped from a distance, roughly between ages sixteen and twenty. The nearest thing to a date we ever had was when I invited her to the Yale prom in my sophomore year, and to the Yale-Harvard football game. She always accepted, but the whole time we were together I was completely tongue-tied. Peggy Ramsey was very shy too, so we would just dance. At the prom in those days you had a dance program that you filled out. Part of taking a girl to the big football game of the year was to present her with a bouquet of violets—the Yale bouquet—which I scrupulously did. Peggy Ramsey was beautiful, misty-eyed. And she had an air of mystery about her, partly because she never said anything. In a sense, she had all that I required: I could imagine her thinking any kind of thought I wished. Her father, an obste-trician, had died several years before I knew her. It was probably more than a coincidence that I imagined Marta to be an orphan, that Peggy was fatherless, and that Jane, my girl from the age of twenty and the one whom I married at twenty-four, was also fatherless. I must have been unconsciously afraid of jealous fathers.

TWO ANDOVER CLASSMATES, Al Wilson and Al Lindley, both went out for crew in our freshman year at Yale. But for some reason, at that point it never occurred to me to do likewise. I went out again for high-jumping, which is not a glorious sport—and, in fact, can be sort of lonely. In the winter I practiced all by myself in a room in the gym that had mats on the floor and a slender bar, which I would jump over and land with a thud on the mat. I stuck with high-jumping because it provided my only athletic identity, though I was not to make an inch of progress in a total of three years, counting Andover. So my freshman year was a disaster I felt I had slipped back to being a wretched outsider.

One day, on my way to the room in the gym where I practiced that winter, I paused to admire the varsity and junior varsity crews rowing on machines under the coaching of the Corderry brothers. (Today the varsity crews practice in a tank with circulating water and real oars.) The man sitting on the bench behind where I was standing turned, looked me up and down, and asked, "What sport do you go out for?" I was overwhelmed to realize that it was Langhorn Gibson, captain of the crew and son of the illustrator Charles Dana Gibson, creator of the "Gibson Girl." He was an imposing figure, with his large head resembling a bust of a Roman senator and his slightly arrogant manner. "High-jumping," I answered, and would have added "sir" if that had been acceptable usage. He said with scorn, "Why don't you go out for a man's sport?" I didn't feel insulted, I was elated—the captain had implied I was possible crew material! I'd known since reading *Stover at Yale* in boyhood that rowing was a noble and glorious sport. I hurried around to the crew office to sign up for spring practice, though it was still two months away.

Yale crews at that time were being trounced by all colleges except

Harvard, but that didn't discourage the flood of candidates. I was assigned to Freshman M, the thirteenth freshman crew. I got no coaching there—the freshman coach was working with the first two or three crews. I knew nothing and learned nothing. I kept one foot in high-jumping for safety and won my class numerals by getting the familiar half-point against the Harvard freshmen.

The varsity crews practiced at Derby, a town fifteen miles outside New Haven on the Housatonic River. There was a dam that provided still water on the river, and a boathouse. That's where the four varsity crews and the two freshman crews practiced. The class crews practiced from a large old boathouse in an industrial region of New Haven Harbor, where the water was dirty and the view was dismal.

That summer between freshman and sophomore years, an important change took place. The Yale Graduate Rowing Committee, tired of unsuccessful crews, hired Ed Leader, the assistant head coach from the University of Washington in Seattle, and he brought about a revolution in rowing that autumn. Until that time most East Coast colleges used the English stroke, which ended with an exaggerated layback. Then it was by a great physical exertion that you hoisted yourself from an almost supine position to a sitting-up and then a bending-forward position. Ed Leader and the other coaches in Washington and California were using a very different stroke in which there was practically no layback at all. But height was necessary in order to get length in the stroke—you had to be at least six feet tall.

As is true in all athletics, it was easier for beginners like me to learn Leader's new stroke than for the experienced oarsmen to unlearn their English style. So all fall and winter there was a filtering down of experienced oarsmen—even from the varsity— who couldn't adapt, and a filtering upward of newcomers. I started the fall on Sophomore D, got some coaching, and applied myself with desperate determination, leapfrogged upward, and made the junior varsity by the time we got on the river in spring.

In its first year under Ed Leader the varsity won all its races handily—this only one year after being beaten by everybody but Harvard. And even with Leader paying most of his attention to the varsity, the junior varsity unexpectedly beat Harvard. I was ecstatic.

Sophomore year was a great leap forward in all respects. When I got on the junior varsity in late winter, I explained to my father that I had to eat all three meals at the training table (I don't think it was really obligatory) and that therefore I had to live at the college; and he and my mother consented to my moving to a room in Wright Hall on the Old Campus.

JUNIOR YEAR was even more dizzying. In the fall I made the varsity. In May I was tapped for the senior society Scroll and Key, which seemed proof that I'd finally become an acceptable fellow, or at least had learned how to act like one. And the Yale crew won the 1924 Olympic Trials in Philadelphia—by only a few feet, but that was enough. Nowadays, to select the Olympic crew, they appoint a coach who observes and tests oarsmen at various colleges and then assembles a crew from the available oarsmen. But in those days it was done by competitions between college crews.

The trip to the Olympic Games in Paris was a succession of delights. The eight-day voyage in first-class on the S.S. *Homeric* (no planes to Europe then) was luxurious in every way except that by Ed's rules we had to go to bed by ten, were held to a rigid training table diet, and practiced rowing on machines installed on an upper deck. (They swung a lifeboat over the side to make room for them.) Ordinarily when you're rowing you are far away from any spectators, so it was exciting to row every morning and every afternoon and have other passengers come and watch us—debutantes were within a couple of feet of us!

We were also allowed to go onto the dance floor every night, as long as we left for bed by ten o'clock. I was on the dance floor every night of the voyage. But once when I was dancing with a girl, it got to be something like five minutes past ten. I didn't know how to excuse myself in the middle of a dance. Ed Leader walked through, saw me on the dance floor, and called a meeting of all the oarsmen the next morning. Seeming very angry, he said that he'd seen me on the dance floor after ten and he wanted it understood that the next time this happened, the offending oarsman would be sent back to the United States on the first boat. Well, all my crew mates looked at me reproachfully as if I had carelessly jeopardized our chances for victory. Later I found out that a number of them had gone on a binge the night before, done some drinking, and ended up with an inspection tour of the bowels of the ship. And they all looked at me as if I were the traitor!

*The 1924 Yale crew. Ben is standing, second from the right;*
*Ed Leader is standing on the far left.*

Gloria Swanson, the reigning Hollywood queen, was on the boat traveling incognito. She rarely appeared in public. The crew managers considered it one of their challenges to try to get her to consent to meet the members of the crew and to dance with each of us briefly. They finally persuaded her. But within a couple of nights she was awakened very late by a steward delivering a mash note from a man who told her that he was madly in love with her, and signed it Eli, which is the nickname for Yale students. She assumed that it was one of the crew who had written this note, was furious at having her sleep disturbed, and canceled the agreement to meet us. The poor managers went to work again and finally persuaded her, and she appeared on the dance floor for about a half-hour. They brought us up one by one to cut in and be introduced to her. The person who had been dancing with her just before me was Archie Quarrier, a genial but sometimes bumbling fellow. (One day near the boathouse on the Seine he was run down by a bicyclist.) When the manager brought me up, Archie, somewhat flustered, grinned sheepishly at me and said, "Big Ben." Gloria Swanson looked at me and without a moment's hesitation, said, "Big Ben but no alarm." This was not exactly flattering to my masculinity, but I was pleased to have her even notice my name and make a personal remark. So I happily danced with her once around the floor. I couldn't think of anything to say and she didn't bother to say anything more, and then a manager cut in with another person.

Perhaps forty years later I was on Mike Douglas's television talk show, and who else should be sitting in the same silly gazebo but Gloria Swanson. While we were waiting for the program to begin, I reminded her that I had met her years before on the S.S. *Homeric*. She immediately—and grumpily—recalled how she had been awakened that night by the mash note from "Eli."

To Ed Leader the trip brought moments of bewilderment as well as mounting anxiety that through some misfortune we would be denied victory. Ed looked like an ex-pugilist with his lumpy, scowling face, piercing eyes, and loud, husky voice. When he was told

VILLAGE OLYMPIQUE.

*The Olympic Village, Paris, 1924.*

that as a first-class passenger on the *Homeric* he must wear a tuxedo to dinner, he exploded with indignation and embarrassment, "What! A goddamned waiter suit!" He was always tense and preoccupied. The only time I remember him relaxing with me was when he looked at my thin behind one day in the shower room and said, "Spock, you don't have an ass. You just have a couple of soda biscuits." Underneath his rough exterior he was kind and ingenuous.

It was agreed, after one breakfast at the Olympic Village consisting of one dry orange the diameter of a fifty-cent piece, a roll, and coffee—in contrast to our usual fruit, cereal, eggs, bacon, stacks of toast, and milk—that we couldn't win or even survive on such a diet. The rowing committee, which had two multimillionaires on it, apparently was supplying us with unlimited funds, so we moved to the handsome old city of Saint Germain-en-Laye outside Paris, where we lived next to a castle with a moat and a forest, and took our meals at a distinguished restaurant, François Premier. When Madame, the proprietress, a husky woman with a black mustache, prepared us a surprise lobster dinner to celebrate the Fourth of July, Ed stared with horror at the heap of lobsters on the platter, which to him meant only the threat of shellfish poisoning, and cried, "Take them away!"

Against his better judgment, he was persuaded to let us attend, on a Sunday, the running of the Grand Prix at the Longchamps racetrack. He shouted after us as we departed, "Don't sit on any stone walls—you'll get piles!" We were dressed in what we then considered high style for summer: white flannel trousers, white buckskin shoes, blue blazers, and boater straw hats. We soon found that we were the only people among fifty thousand spectators to be dressed that way, and we felt like clowns. Ordinary Frenchmen then wore black suits and black Homburg hats in all seasons, and the French and English horsey swells were in gray cutaways with gray top hats.

The crew was obliged to take afternoon naps while at Saint Germain-en-Laye. Our captain, who had met and fallen in love with a fellow passenger during our transatlantic voyage, would slip out for a rendezvous and dignified promenade with this girl, whose proper mother brought her out daily by taxi from Paris. One day he miscalculated the time and was not in our bus, a white open model like a huge bathtub, when it was time to depart for the Seine. In fact, he could be seen a block away, saying goodbye. Ed Leader rose wrathfully from his seat and bellowed down the block, "You should be ashamed of yourself! The crew is ready for practice, and where is the captain? On a street corner talking to a *woman*!" He spat out the word as if she were a tramp.

On the day of the final race, as we carried our shell down to the float, we saw Ed Leader towering over the gentlemanly English coxswain and thundering at him, "Don't you foul us, do you understand? Don't you foul us!" Just such an incident had happened in the preliminary heat the day before. If one boat gets slightly off course and its oars get tangled with those of another boat, neither boat can extricate itself; they must drift apart. Ed had lain awake all that night worrying that such a mishap might happen to our boat. Al Lindley, our stroke, usually imperturbable, had apparently also stayed awake all night worrying, so at the end of the race he collapsed well beyond the usual point of exhaustion. We had paused in front of the grandstand where we received our applause and were then supposed to row away. The applause died down, but we had to stay and stay—a full ten minutes!—until Al recovered. We won by over three boat lengths, a disgraceful margin for a race of 2,000 meters—only a mile and a quarter.

We hadn't arrived in Paris in time for the opening ceremonies; we'd had to stay behind to row against Harvard while the rest of the Olympic team sailed over on the S.S. *United States*. And when we came back, since it was still the middle of summer, there wasn't a soul on campus to welcome us back—nothing until a big athletics banquet put on by New York alumni, after the football team's successful season. They took over half the seats in a big Broadway show and got the cast to modify some of the songs to reflect our presence. Yale men. That was our only official celebration.

Many, many years later I saw the film *Chariots of Fire*, which is, of course, about the 1924 Olympic Games. I was inspired by it, though I hadn't actually known any of the American runners. We didn't compete near the track or the field, and we lived by ourselves in a different town. We only saw oarsmen from other countries toward the very end, at the semifinals and the finals. We were not in the same athletic circles at all.

B Y MY JUNIOR YEAR at Yale, I was majoring in English and minoring in history. Many people going into medicine major in chemistry and biology. I think that it's a big mistake to try to get into medical school by spending all your time in college taking such courses. Medicine is a narrowing profession as it is; it tends

JEUX OLYMPIQUES DE 1924 AVIRON
LE HUIT DES ÉTATS-UNIS

*The Yale crew rowing on the Seine.*

to absorb all the interest and drive of most physicians. The undergraduate years may be the last chance to get a broader glimpse of what life and the world are about. I'm glad that it was not hard to get into medical school, and that I could major in English.

One of my most interesting courses at Yale was one in ancient Greek literature taught by a broadly educated young Greek named Aristides Phoutrides. When he would compare certain works of Greek, American, and English literature, he saw the blank look on our faces and would ask, "Haven't you read Dreiser?" And every person in the class shook his head. He was shocked at our ignorance.

Mr. Phoutrides drowned while sailing in Maine on summer vacation. I felt the loss and the fear. I have always been afraid of drowning. Maybe that's why I love sailing: because it is counterphobic. I sail in order to show the ocean I can outwit it.

During senior year I enjoyed the fruits of my successes. Yet I felt secret embarrassment at how grimly I'd worked toward them— and not for God, for country, or for Yale, as the song goes, but for release from my self-image as a mother's boy. The way it happened, though, I was able to close the ledger of my undergraduate years quite cheerfully, thanks really to Ed Leader's new stroke, and to turn my mind to medicine and the outside world.

*Relaxing on an ocean liner en route to France, following graduation from Yale.*

*Working the gravel under the ties on the Canadian Pacific Railroad.*
*The assistant foreman is in the foreground.*

# 7

ALL THROUGH BOARDING SCHOOL and college I had a variety of summer jobs: at the newsboys' camp after my junior year at Andover, counselor at the Newington Crippled Children's Home after each of three years at Yale—which is probably what solidified my idea of going to medical school.

After my first year of medical school the Bureau of Appointments at Yale had offered me one job I immediately accepted. It was to be tutor/companion to a boy of ten or twelve in Southampton, a plush summer community on the Long Island shore. I would be given two days off per week, have a car at my disposal, and be paid several times more than at the Crippled Children's Home.

I went home in triumph. It wasn't just the cushy job—I craved the romantic life: parties, yacht clubs, country clubs. It was just the kind of place I wanted to go to as a youth, and just the kind of place my mother abhorred. When I told her about the job, she landed on me like a ton of bricks. "You should be ashamed of yourself, wanting to be nursemaid to a rich boy!"

She still had such control over my conscience that I went down the next day to the Bureau of Appointments and said, "I've changed my mind on the job at Southampton. What's the hardest job you've got?" This was clearly masochism, to go even further in self-denial than my mother asked. They explained that there was a job that nobody wanted. It was with Frontier College in Winnipeg, Canada, which was run by two retired clergymen. The job was to teach the English language and Canadian customs to immigrants. There were hundreds of thousands of them in Canada who took the jobs that no one else wanted, most of them seasonal: frequently at lumber camps in winter, on railroad extra gangs in spring, then in the wheatfields in August. Frontier College's idea was that before you can effectively teach them Canadian customs and English, you must earn their respect by working with them ten hours a day. Needless to say, that part seemed like the bigger job.

They assigned me to Joe Contini's extra gang. Canadian Pacific Railroad pay was thirty cents an hour, and the regular workday was ten hours. You would earn three dollars a day, turn back one dollar for a bunk and board, and keep two. But if it rained and you didn't work, you still had to pay the dollar a day. So when the harvest came in, there was no hesitation about dropping the railroad—you could get *five dollars* a day at the harvest, and this seemed like fantastic riches, for a few weeks' work.

As an academic institution I was a failure. The first night I had practically the whole gang of about forty men, almost entirely Galicians from a region between Poland and Hungary, and I started with a chart showing pictures of knives, forks, and spoons. The second night I had about a third of the gang, the third night about five men, and after that only one, a Cockney Englishman who wanted to be my friend. The Galicians had been curious about English and what Canadian customs might be, but they weren't serious about needing that knowledge. They'd go to the railroad as a gang, then to the harvest as a gang, and then to the lumber camps as a gang. They would stop to see their wives and children in a city somewhere for a few days in between jobs, and they wouldn't use English.

Railroad tracks are generally taken care of by what's called a

*Working on the Canadian Pacific.*

section gang. The length of the section of track assigned to a gang depends partly on the conditions there, how hard it is to maintain the track. And in western Ontario it was very hard on track, being muskeg, or swamp, country. To build a railroad there, in the beginning they dumped what they call gravel (really just sand and stones) and set the ties and tracks on that. You could actually watch it getting out of condition: as a train went by, the truck of each car would momentarily press the track down a few inches, slightly compacting the gravel and displacing it off to the side. Over the months the track got undulating waves in it and the two sets of track slid sideways, away from each other. The work in a place like that was too much for a section gang, so an extra gang would be sent in.

Their main job was straightening track, and they used two tools, a shovel and a tamping bar. They went along the edge of the roadbed—about eight men to a rail—and shoveled the gravel up on top of the ties, between the rails; then they would jack up the tracks and eight men would work the gravel down under the ties by rotating the shovel handle in a circle and scrunching the blade in the gravel with a horrible squeaking noise. After that, another team of eight men would pack the gravel tighter under the tie with long, heavy tamping bars.

After a few dozen ties had been raised, the whole gang would line up along the two rails with long crowbars. At the assistant foreman's cry "Yo *heava!*" they would give a short heave and the whole track would move sideways a few inches. The foreman would lie on his belly on the track, watching to see when it got set straight, while the assistant kept up the rhythmic cry.

I was assigned to a shovel to throw the gravel up from the edge of the roadbed. From my point of view, this was the most difficult job (though the foreman had given it to me on the assumption that you don't have to know much to be able to shovel). The trouble was, these shovels had very short handles, so I had to bend double to get my shovel down to the ground and I stayed bent double for hours. And it was very hard to shovel that mixture of sand and stones because you'd try to thrust your shovel in and it would just bang into a rock, squeak, and stop. There was some kind of magic that you learned after a while, a way of thrusting the shovel in and wiggling it around in the gravel at the same time. Well, within an hour my back would be so stiff and aching that I couldn't stand up. I don't remember whether the foreman saw that I was in misery or whether I begged for another job, but anyway he put me on a tamping bar.

Toward the end of the summer I got promoted to a choice job called "bull cook," setting the long tables and carrying bowls of food from the cook car—neither of which has anything to do with cooking. My main job was to take care of the sleeping cars, the ancient, tiny boxcars they lived in, sweeping them out and sort of tidying them up. In each car there was a tin basin and a great big pitcher, which they would use to wash themselves. Each man would pour a little water in the basin and splash himself the way a bird does. I had to go get water for the men and for the cook, sometimes a couple of miles down the track, and for this I would use a handcar, which was fun to operate.

The third job I hate to mention, because I failed at it: flagman. When the crew went out in the morning on handcars to work on a piece of track, a flagman had to be two miles away to stop any approaching train or at least slow it way down. You would put two torpedos on the track, six feet apart. As a locomotive hit the torpedo it made a loud bang, so that the engineer was alerted. You're standing there beside the track with a red flag, and you make one signal or another, either to stop or to slow way down. I'd earned that job by staying longer than almost anyone else on the gang— three months altogether.

The ordinary freight trains were of lowest importance on the railroad. Then came passenger trains, including the transcontinental express. Most important were the stock trains that carried cattle from west to east. They had limited water and food, and these trains must not be delayed long or else the cattle would begin dying. So the rule was: Don't delay the stock train.

One day the gang was working on the eastbound track, a mile east of our boxcars. So I was told to walk one mile west of the boxcars and take up my flagman's position. Always before, the foreman had told me in such situations to pick up the torpedos at a quarter of twelve and start walking back to our cars for lunch, because by then the track would be in usable condition. This morning he forgot to instruct me. The stock train was expected at eleven o'clock. But at eleven it hadn't come, and at half past it hadn't come. And I was worrying what to do. It got to be a quarter to twelve, and off in the distance I heard the whistle of the stock train. Which is my duty? I kept asking myself. I was sure the track

*Ben on Joe Contini's extra gang.*

would be in shape by now, so I took the torpedos off the track.

That turned out to be the wrong thing to do. The track *was* in good condition. But the foreman had decided to have the handcars use the eastbound track returning to the camp as being safer, in view of the blind curve between the two locations, on the assumption that I would be slowing the stock train. So the stock train and the handcars were heading for each other on the same track. They didn't get much warning: they had to stop the handcars, jump off, and lift the handcars off the track.

As I walked into view, I thought the men were giving me black looks, but maybe it was my guilty conscience. I told the foreman, "I don't want to be flagman anymore." He said, "It's all right, it's all right," meaning that it was also his fault and I had learned my lesson, but I said, "No, no! I don't want to be flagman anymore!"

Was I happy when that summer ended! On top of it all, I'd lost my felt hat. In the 1920s everyone wore a felt hat, even college men. So when I got to the first city in Canada where I was changing trains, I bought myself a new felt hat. Not till I got to the East did I realize that I had lost my eye for hats—it was a Western type and much too wide in the brim. I was fascinated that in only three months' time my judgment in clothes had disappeared.

*Jane and Ben on their honeymoon, 1927.*

# 8

MY GRADE AVERAGE for my four undergraduate years at Yale was C+. A "gentleman's C" they used to call it. But they never questioned that at Yale Medical School. There was no competitive push of students then from a college like Yale to get into medical school, so they were willing to take anybody who could pass the prerequisite courses and was not a reprobate. Yale was a good medical school, but still it was dull stuff compared to the exciting academic, social, and athletic life of my undergraduate years. And as if that weren't depressing enough, I also had to move back home. I found it very difficult to study. At the end of the afternoon I would go home and jog around the neighborhood because Ed Leader had said it was important to keep exercising. I'd have dinner with my parents and return to my room.

Yale Medical School had a very progressive philosophy. You didn't have to take any examinations for two years unless you wanted to. But I still didn't do very well academically. I remember the gloom I felt during my first year, sitting in my room at night with *Gray's Anatomy* open before me. We started with the clavicle, the collarbone. There were a certain number of surfaces on the clavicle, one for this muscle and another for that muscle, and there were joints at the ends. I thought, Who *cares* about the clavicle and how many surfaces there are on it? If I were going to be a surgeon, no doubt I would need to know about the clavicle. But as a first-year medical student I couldn't imagine anything less appealing. So it was not surprising that when I took examinations at the end of two years, I just squeaked by.

My parents had always expected me to work hard and do my best at school. On the other hand, when I got poor grades they didn't scold me or say I had to do better. My father never said that he would like me to go into the law because he did. They both respected my decision to go to medical school to become a pediatrician, though even I had little idea of what exactly I was getting into, or what the differences were between, say, a pediatrician, a pediatric surgeon, and an orthopedist.

B ACK IN 1923, as a sophomore on the junior varsity crew that had unexpectedly beat Harvard, I was exultant inside but still extremely shy with girls. The weekend after the races, in the backseat of a car going to a party, I tried to hold a girl's hand and she snatched it away; I didn't try again for months. But at a dance at Black Point, Connecticut, the same weekend, I gave a big rush to Cynthia Cheney, whom I took to be an "older woman," of perhaps twenty-seven. Tolerantly amused, I thought, by the attentions of a twenty-year-old boy, she said nothing while we were dancing (I wasn't brave enough to start a conversation), but she did smile every time I cut back in. Eventually I discovered she was fifteen and too scared and inexperienced to make small talk.

Later in the summer she invited me to Black Point for the Labor Day weekend. There I met her sister, Jane, who was eighteen and had a very different personality: serious-minded, earnest in her conversation, interested in psychology enough to have volunteered at a child guidance clinic. She immediately took me over for the long weekend, and we drove together from one activity or party to another. Much later she explained that she hadn't felt guilty about stealing me from Cynthia; Cynthia was just too young. (They were deeply rivalrous.)

For the first time in my life I was being taken seriously by an attractive girl who wanted to exchange thoughts with me, and I was delighted. Intoxicated, in fact—I hardly noticed I was neglecting Cynthia. That fall I invited Jane to the Yale-Harvard football game and the dance the night before. She had already accepted an invitation to the game with a friend of mine, but I persuaded her to go with me to the dance anyway. This aggressive interference with a friend's weekend date shows how determined I could be when I got going. I also became ruthless about the prom in February. I'd already invited Peggy Ramsey, but then I asked another friend to take her over so that I could invite Jane. And at the dinner party at our house before the dance, I had the nerve to seat Jane and Peggy flanking me, like a sultan with two favorites.

It was an on-again-off-again but still intense relationship for the next two years—my junior and senior years at Yale, Jane's freshman and sophomore years at Bryn Mawr. With classic male egotism, I wanted Jane to date no one but me. Yet I was offering nothing more than a yearly football game, prom, and boat race, with some letters in between. She would say, quite sensibly, that she needed to know a variety of men. In a huff I'd call our relationship off, though I'd still be thinking of her a great deal. Then when we'd get together in South Manchester (where her very extended Cheney family had been making silk for generations) or in Bryn Mawr or New York, the old magic would take hold. And then I'd get jealous and huffy again.

We had a crucial rendezvous at Black Point in the summer of 1925 just before Jane, Cynthia, and their mother left for France (it had long been planned that Jane would go to Bryn Mawr for only two years, then to France for one year). The prospect of the separation drew us together and made us drop the nonsense of the old quarrels. We were committed, though not even our families knew. We regularly wrote long letters that started and ended with messages of love and were packed in between with the observations of a first-year medical student in America and an American girl in Paris.

By the time Jane was back from France and I was in my second year of medical school, we wanted to get married and move to New York. New Haven seemed dull, conventional, too full of my family's friends. Most of my college friends were now in New York. So I applied to the College of Physicians and Surgeons at Columbia University and was accepted.

I sold my father a bill of goods, I think, in getting him to let me transfer to Physicians and Surgeons. For one thing, the tuition there was over six hundred dollars, about three times as much as at Yale Medical School. My father was even more stunned when I told him I wanted to get married. "What on?" he said, meaning how did I propose to maintain myself and a wife. A good question.

My mother had been in favor of my engagement and marriage. She was against long engagements. Her only reservation had been that when Jane came down to attend a fancy-dress ball in New Haven, she wore a Spanish shawl off one shoulder. My mother thought that was risqué, and my little sister Sally asked her when she was going to put her dress on. Nevertheless, Jane and I got married that June in a Cheney garden.

We both thought New York was wonderful; everywhere else seemed small-time. This was emancipation, and Greenwich Village represented the essence of the New York we were after, not the grand part but a cultural center, where restless, ambitious, curious people go to expand their horizons. Our first apartment—a small place with no space left unused—was at 19 West 8th Street in a brownstone house over a storefront, like the rest of the block. As a youth in New Haven, I'd once been sent to deliver a message to a cleaning woman and found her living over a store—a sad state of affairs, I thought at the time. But now it seemed quite the New York thing to do. When Jane and I were still looking, and we inquired of a potential neighbor about the hot water and other services, she assured us that everything was in order—and addressed us as "Dear." Coming from a stranger, this seemed a surprising but friendly gesture that we would not have encountered in our hometowns. It seemed part of the freedom and intimacy of the place.

My father had agreed to pay my tuition. Jane expected to get her allowance from her mother, some two thousand dollars a year, and she got a job that paid an equal amount, taking family histories of patients at the Constitution Clinic at Presbyterian Hospital. I had a five-thousand-dollar legacy from my godfather, and we'd received a couple of thousand dollars as wedding presents. We found that we could live on two hundred dollars a month. Even paying seventy-five dollars a month for rent, we were saving money. We were *very* frugal.

In those years, of course, a dollar still went a long way: a decent lunch of several courses could be had for a dollar and a quarter at a modest restaurant. But Jane and I felt we couldn't afford to eat out at all. Jane cooked, and we would spend only twenty-five cents for the meat—usually top round, which looks good in the store but is actually a tough cut. Once we invited Judge and Mrs. Learned Hand for dinner, but all we felt we could afford to serve was spaghetti.

We kept meticulous accounts, down to two cents a day for the *New York Times*. Jane's most beautiful evening dress cost fifteen dollars at a sale at Macy's. We did the laundry in the bathtub using a device that churned the water around. Jane ironed the collars and cuffs of my shirts by stretching them wet over the rim of the tub; the rumpled remainder of the shirts would be conveniently hidden by my jacket and vest.

A T YALE it hadn't seemed peculiar that there were no women or blacks and that the few Jews there were discriminated against socially. I didn't have any sense of civil rights. I took it for granted that you went to school with people of your own sex, of your own kind. That was just the way things were. It wasn't until

I transferred to Physicians and Surgeons that I first heard opinions different from the ones in my family, different from what my friends at Yale talked about, and I began to question these and other matters.

While I was an undergraduate at Yale, where nine out of ten undergraduates were highly conservative and strictly apolitical, I don't remember ever having a political discussion. When I got to Columbia, I was greatly surprised to find that some students were avowed Democrats, a few even Socialists. My father had given me the idea that no university graduate would be a Democrat. As he put it, the Republicans create all the wealth in the United States, and the Democrats, incapable of creating wealth or anything else, use politics to try to cut a slice for themselves.

As a lawyer, eventually general counsel, for the New Haven Railroad, my father was politically very conservative, and a Republican—he would have added, "Of course." A railroad lawyer's job was to fight off attempts by the federal Interstate Commerce Commission to control the railroads, which had been largely owned by robber barons like J. P. Morgan and Commodore Vanderbilt. When my father took me to the polls in my senior year in college (1924), he declared that Calvin Coolidge, the Republican incumbent, was the greatest president the United States ever had. Only later did I understand that he thought so because Coolidge's sentiments about business were very much my father's: that the least government is the best government, that the business of America is business.

To have my preconceptions challenged as they were at Columbia stirred me up, and gradually from 1927 on—especially after the crash of 1929—I was discussing politics with anybody who was willing. Without quite realizing what I was doing, I always took conservative Republican positions when arguing with my more liberal medical-school friends who gave me liberal and radical arguments, but in the evening I found myself using *their* arguments against my conservative undergraduate friends. I kept this up for about five years.

The illogic of arguing both sides didn't occur to me until I was in psychoanalytic training around 1934, and Dr. Feigenbaum, one of my mentors, happened to remark that if you believe something you don't have to argue. I had thought you argued to convert somebody to your belief. But he was pointing out the more dynamic position: the impulse to argue comes from ambivalent feelings about the issues. Certainly, I was a prime example of this. I used to say to Jane, "Why is it that everywhere I go, people want to argue politics and economics with me?" Of course, I was provoking them. When they made the slightest reference to politics or economics I would launch into a strenuous argument. It's a wonder that I had any friends left.

This continual debating in which I played devil's advocate resolved itself in my becoming a Democrat. By 1928 I was ready to vote not for Hoover but for Al Smith, even though he was a Catholic, which was deemed highly unsuitable (and even though my father had once related with great scorn that throughout a meeting where both were present, Smith was paring his nails—the height of vulgarity). Herbert Hoover's performance in office, I felt, revealed his bleak lack of courage and understanding in dealing with everything from growing unemployment to the "noble experiment" of Prohibition. I could scarcely avoid having a political attitude after the Depression set in, what with friends becoming unemployed and people having fewer babies, it certainly affected my pediatric practice. So I became a "New Deal" liberal. I admired Franklin Roosevelt and agreed with his methods of employing people through government projects, all the way from sweeping up parks to painting murals in post offices.

THERE WAS NOTHING PROGRESSIVE about the medical education at Columbia. I took examinations every few weeks and memorized in preparation for them. We had a group that studied together. One person in the group was able to get hold of every examination from the years before, so we got a very good idea of what kind of questions would be asked on each exam, and we were primed and ready. My classmates were as surprised as I was when I ended up leading the class at the end of the third and fourth years. This was an example of what motivation will do: I was away from my former family, I was a married man on my way to a career, I felt responsible for Jane and myself.

In our senior year at Columbia, when plans were discussed to drop Bellevue Hospital as a training facility for Columbia students, I organized a petition against this. At Bellevue the staff treated the students with respect and encouragement, as if they were pleased to be teaching us. At Presbyterian we had to ask a student nurse to chaperone us whenever we examined a woman patient, and often she would say snippily, "I don't have time!" The interns, residents, and attending physicians also often seemed too busy to teach us. All the students signed the petition to the dean of the medical school requesting that Bellevue not be eliminated, which succeeded. At Yale Medical School there had been an idealistic philosophy among the faculty that all of us—faculty as well as students—were studying medicine together. At Physicians and Surgeons there was no such talk. We were the students, and the faculty in the last two (clinical) years consisted mainly of practitioners who, for the prestige and other advantages of being on a medical-school faculty, consented to enlighten the students.

Since I had gone to medical school to be a pediatrician, I didn't have to wait to decide on my specialty. In different parts of the country the most common way of becoming a pediatrician was to take a year of rotating internship, then a residency for two or three years in pediatrics. But some older, successful pediatricians I knew in New York told me they had started out by training in medicine first, and that made me want to do the same thing. The most sought after position to get was the two-year internship in either medicine or surgery at Presbyterian Hospital in New York City, which was intimately connected with Columbia. I applied and got a medical internship for the years 1929 to 1931.

Our training was very careful and very thorough. We were paid nothing and had every other night off if our work was done. I was certainly not a first-class intern. I seemed to have no time to read the medical literature and was not always caught up in my work. I was something of a procrastinator.

In 1928 Columbia's medical school moved from 59th Street opposite Roosevelt Hospital to Broadway at 168th Street in Washington Heights, much farther uptown. Presbyterian Hospital went there too. Jane and I soon followed them to the new neighborhood, prompted by the collapse of the ceiling in our Greenwich Village apartment.

Nobody on the staff liked the new Presbyterian Hospital at first. It had lost its intimacy in the move and seemed too large, too modern, too impersonal. In the old Presbyterian, at Park Avenue in the seventies, interns and residents had dined with the attending physicians; now they were relegated to a huge general cafeteria quite audibly close to the dishwashing facility. The meals were poor too. The worst was lunch on Wednesdays, which consisted of a slice of orange-colored but tasteless cheese for protein, two Saltine crackers for starch, and two slices of pale tomato for a vegetable. All the interns and residents at Presbyterian, Babies Hospital, and the Squire Clinic complained bitterly. So Norton Brown, a fellow intern, and I composed a petition to the trustees. It caused indignation because we had bypassed the administration; they wanted to know who had composed it, but nobody squealed. We got better food, and they closed in our dining room, painted it hunter green, and hung hunting prints on the walls.

One night when I was on duty in the emergency room, a mother came in distraught with her eight-month-old baby and said that the baby had swallowed the safety pin from the diaper. While changing the diaper, she had taken out the pin, laid it down, and turned to get out a fresh diaper. She had looked for the pin and it wasn't there, so she *knew* the baby had swallowed it. She was crying hysterically, though obviously the baby was quite comfortable.

To reassure her, I suggested that we fluoroscope the baby. We went into the fluoroscope room, laid the baby down on the table, turned off the light, and turned on the fluoroscope. I brought the screen down over the baby's head and pointed out to the mother, "See, there's the skull, there's the mouth, there's the throat, and there's the chest—and there's no sign of a safety pin." As we got to the lower abdomen, into view came a *huge* safety pin. It looked as big as one used on a horse blanket because it was distorted and enlarged by its relationship to the fluoroscope screen.

The mother screamed and fainted dead away on the floor. I then realized that this safety pin we saw was the one on the baby's diaper. The mother had used another safety pin on the diaper before bringing the baby to the hospital, and I hadn't taken off the diaper to fluoroscope the baby. After reviving the mother, I tried to explain this to her, but she thought that I was just giving her meaningless sweet talk.

At Presbyterian we had people from all economic backgrounds. The outpatients, mostly from Washington Heights, a predominantly lower-middle-class Jewish neighborhood, were generally very intelligent, even when not particularly well educated. This was in contrast to the clientele at New York Nursery and Child Hospital, where I followed my two years at Presbyterian with a one-year residency in pediatrics. The hospital was at 10th Avenue and West 60th Street, in the neighborhood then well named Hell's Kitchen.

Poor, uneducated, often demoralized parents would, for example, bring in their babies suffering from chronic diarrhea from spoiled milk. The parents had no way to refrigerate milk except by putting the bottles out on the windowsill in the winter. We would cure the diarrhea with water and intravenous fluids, but within a few weeks the baby would be brought back for the same thing.

The hospital building itself was old and dingy, with six or eight floors of obstetrics and only one of pediatrics. But it had been the main pediatric teaching service for Cornell Medical College, and long ago the famous Henry Holt had been chief of the pediatric service. I'd selected this pediatric service because within a year it would be part of the new New York Hospital–Cornell Medical Center going up in the East 60s, which seemed far more practical than getting attached to Babies Hospital at West 168th Street, a half-hour trip by car from the East 70s, where I wanted my office.

SOMETIME during the pediatric residency years (1931–1932) I conceived the idea that someone going into pediatrics should have psychological training. I already knew in a vague way that parents would be asking about toilet training and thumb-sucking and resistance to weaning, about fears, about sibling rivalry . . . Questions like these had been coming up in pediatric practice for a long time, but pediatricians just used traditional answers like the one for thumb-sucking: It's a bad habit. You try to break the habit by painting nasty stuff on the baby's thumbs or by enclosing his hands in aluminum mitts or by spread-eagling him, tying his wrists to the side of the crib. I knew that these methods were wrong, but I didn't know what was right.

I asked a few pediatricians in New York about psychological training for pediatric practice. They said there was no such training in New York. I wrote to three pediatricians in other parts of the United States. All three said there was no such thing. It never occurred to me to go to a department of psychology in a university— when you are in the medical groove, you think only in terms of medical residencies.

So I consulted the people who were selecting residents in psychiatry for Payne Whitney Clinic, which would be part of the new complex of New York Hospital–Cornell. They said that one floor at Payne Whitney would be given over to children's psychiatry. My hope was that half of my patients would be children.

As it turned out, they had actually very few children's cases. In the ten months I spent there, I got just two. Most of my patients were adults suffering from manic-depressive psychosis or schizophrenia. For a couple of months I had an eight-year-old patient,

*Ben Spock with fellow interns from Presbyterian Hospital, 1930.*

a sociopath who had been moved around from one foster home to another and was overactive and uncontrollable. She was a handful, and I'd had no experience in dealing with such problem children. The residents' offices were very elegant, with carpeting and fine mahogany desks. In my beautiful office this child was into everything, just bouncing around like a drop of water on a hot stove. There was a bottle of ink in the drawer, and she immediately discovered it . . . I knew I shouldn't be a scold or a jailer, so I spent my time gently restraining her.

The residency at Payne Whitney gave me little of what I needed. I wanted to know how to advise parents in practical problems. Taking care of schizophrenic and manic-depressive patients wasn't at all what I needed. But I did learn two things: First, to listen to patients and their relatives. You don't dismiss psychiatric patients because you think they or their families are uncooperative. You are responsible and must deal with them. (Pediatric residents were known to discharge a patient because the parents were uncooperative.) Second, I learned that the staff members at Payne Whitney who could make sense out of the psychotic patients' behavior and talk were those who had had Freudian psychoanalytic training. So I resolved to get that training for myself at the same time I was to start pediatric practice.

*Caroline Zachry, wise educator.*

# 9

AFTER MY RESIDENCY at Payne Whitney Clinic I went into private pediatric practice and did outpatient clinic work in both pediatrics and child psychiatry on the attending staff at New York Hospital. (A couple of years later the new head of psychiatry, interviewing each member of the staff, told me, "This is most unacademic—you will have to choose!" What reactionary nonsense!) I was ready to settle on pediatrics.

My first office was at 215 East 72nd—a very proper building—with a separate entrance on the street. I shared a consulting room and the services of a nurse/receptionist with another pediatrician, Clement B.P. Cobb. The whole office belonged to an obstetrician, Everett Bunzel. I was in practice for three years before I was earning enough to pay my office rent of a hundred twenty-five dollars a month.

As I approached private practice and friends asked me where I expected to get patients, I told them solemnly that I thought it was unwise to have friends for patients, because it might interfere with good pediatric advice and might well disturb your friendship. That was a pompous and unrealistic thing to say, because referrals from physicians were scarce and a good proportion of my patients were children of friends. I was surprised, though, about which friends brought their children to me and which ones didn't.

My first patient parent was Cynthia Colt, whom we had met while spending the summer at Matunuck, Rhode Island. (Jane and I both came from families that always took summer vacations at the shore—affordably or not!) Mrs. Colt telephoned on my first day in the office, the day after Labor Day 1933, and said she'd like to bring in her three daughters—when could she have an appointment? Since I had no other appointments at all, I could have said, "Come right over," but I thought it sounded better to say, "How about day after tomorrow?" I gave them *lots* of attention.

My standard rate for a return office visit was five dollars, an hourlong first visit ten dollars, and a house visit ten, though I'd drop the rate for people who were in less than ideal circumstances. All pediatricians made house visits for illness then, and I was willing to go anywhere to accommodate a patient—even, in one case, to the outermost reaches of Brooklyn. The mother called me one day to say that her fifteen-month-old had turned into a willful devil completely beyond her control. She was distraught so I traveled all the way out to her apartment. We were sitting in the living room when her son toddled into the room. Right away she warned him, in a stern, loud voice, "Now, don't go near the radio!" He stopped cold, then began to edge slowly sideways, toward the radio eyeing his mother all the time. I realized that in her anxiety about not being able to control him, she was inviting the very defiance she feared. They turn up in *Baby and Child Care*.

In 1935 I was offered the part-time job of school physician at Brearley, a private girls' school in Manhattan, and I accepted promptly, as a source of income and a resource for learning. I spent an hour each morning in an office there, checking up on girls returning from illnesses, having conferences with teachers about problem children. The teachers, especially in the lower school, taught me much about differences in behavior at different ages— and at the same age. I also learned about parents. One day I sent home a girl who had impetigo. Immediately her mother rang up the head of the school, demanding furiously that I be removed for suggesting the unthinkable—a filth disease!

The same year, since my summer pediatric practice was paying almost nothing, I took a summer job as doctor at Honnedaga, one of the three summer communities that made up the Adirondack League Club. We went every summer until 1944, when I entered the Navy. Honnedaga was on a remote lake where they needed a doctor for first aid and to get patients to Utica if they had a serious illness like appendicitis. They gave us a tiny cottage right next to the clubhouse. It had a bedroom in front and the office in back. The cottage and all meals were free, and I was able to keep any money I made from house calls or office visits.

Each summer I took in perhaps a hundred dollars in fees, mostly from one patient, let's call her Mrs. Lansing, who was a determined woman. Every summer, as soon as she came up there, the clear, high atmosphere would go to her head and she would go out and

*The doctor's cottage and office, Honnedaga Lake, in the Adirondacks.*

*Morning tennis, Honnedaga Lake.*

walk longer than she was meant to. Then she or her husband would start to worry and ask me to come over after lunch and take her blood pressure. Sure enough, it would always have gone sky-high. And the next day Mr. Lansing would ask me to come over again after lunch, and so on for a week or two till her blood pressure gradually worked down. So I'd say of the hundred dollars that I earned each summer, sixty to seventy dollars was for taking Mrs. Lansing's blood pressure.

THROUGHOUT this period I was also making contact with some people who were to exert a greater or lesser influence on my efforts to find links between pediatrics child development, and the principles of psychoanalysis.

David Levy was first trained as a pediatrician in New York City and then moved over into child psychiatry and child analysis. He contributed two related concepts about thumb-sucking (which was of great concern to most parents in those days and therefore to me): that it was caused by too infrequent feedings at the breast or bottle, and that it also had to do with the total number of minutes per twenty-four hours of nursing, which tended to decrease as the baby got stronger and the rubber nipples softer with age. At the point where a baby could finish in ten minutes a bottle that it had previously taken twenty minutes to finish, thumb-sucking might appear. He experimented with a litter of puppies and fed half of them with medicine droppers instead of letting them nurse from the mother dog. These puppies sucked their own paws or one another's paws and hides until they were partly denuded of hair. Since then I've told parents, and written in *Baby and Child Care*, that one cause of thumb-sucking is insufficient sucking time. When a baby grows strong enough and the nipple grows weak enough so that he can finish a bottle in ten minutes, it's time to buy a new set of nipples.

In 1933, at the same time I began practice, I became a student at the New York Psychoanalytic Institute. This involved a year of analysis with Bertram Lewin and five years of seminars, two a week, half of them from Sandor Rado, the director of the institute. I liked the way Rado always made his points crystal-clear. In 1941 I decided to have another year of analysis with Rado. My unassertive manner was bothering me and I think I hoped that Rado's assertiveness would rub off on me during psychoanalysis.

After the year of analysis with Lewin and a couple of evening seminars, I was told that I could go ahead and analyze a patient, under close supervision. My patient, referred to me from Payne Whitney's outpatient clinic, was a young woman about my age. She was an indignant feminist at a time when feminism had no widespread support. She was unhappy in her professional life because, I would say, of her bitter rivalry with men. Each week I went over with Rado the material from our five sessions. But the analysis was blocked by the patient's rivalry with me. Over a three-year period we did not make significant progress. If I had been able to help that unhappy person change into a happy one, I might have shifted to the psychoanalysis of adults or children. But having discovered how difficult that is, and also how grateful mothers were to have a pediatrician who was willing to spend any amount of time discussing everyday problems of child care, I had no trouble deciding in the end to remain in pediatrics.

The seminars at the institute were orthodox Freudian. Up to that time, my exposure to Freud had been sketchy. In my one psychology course, in the first year of medical school, there had been an isolated lecture on Freud but without any exploration or development of his ideas. I didn't really begin to consider psychoanalysis until my year of psychiatric residency. Staff members would listen to our case reports and it was the psychoanalysts on the staff who made these discussions meaningful. Now at the institute I was getting closer to what I was after, but still no one could tell me what advice I should be giving to parents.

A fellow student at the institute was Caroline Zachry, an educational psychologist, from whom I learned a great deal. Plump and grave, with a slightly squeaky voice, she had a self-assurance that inspired confidence. She taught in a reasonable, unargumentative manner; and from her experience of half a lifetime (she was slightly older than I) she knew every aspect of education inside out. She was a friend of and introduced me to Margaret Mead and Erik Erikson.

Caroline Zachry was originally a student of John Dewey and a leader of the progressive education movement. When I first met her in the early 1930s, she was a student at the New York Psychoanalytic Institute, crossing over into the field of psychoanalysis. This was a bold thing to do, because at the time most of the psychoanalytic societies (certainly that one) were opposed to teaching psychoanalysis to nonmedical people.

Caroline was running a small weekly seminar—her characteristic way of teaching—called "The Institute on Personality Development." It was open to anybody who was interested, but it was designed particularly for schoolteachers, school nurses, pediatricians, and pediatric dentists. It would have been useful for child psychiatrists or child analysts, though I don't remember any being there. Caroline appointed me a leader in the seminar, and I helped to lead the discussion. But more important, I was learning.

In the seminar sessions one person, most often a schoolteacher, would describe a problem child in her class and tell as much as she knew about the child's background. Then the case was open—for questions, for speculation about the dynamics (on this topic the leaders joined in), for listing further information desired, and for suggestions on management. Almost invariably, the first such suggestion would be to refer the child to a psychiatrist or child guidance clinic for evaluation and therapy. And almost invariably Caroline would put the brakes on this suggestion by saying, "Perhaps, at some later point," because to make that decision at the outset would have short-circuited our discussion of all other aspects of management. Then, on the basis of known facts plus sensible speculation, we would discuss what attitude and what methods the teacher might use to help the child in school, what information from the parents and from last year's teacher about the child's past or present adjustment might throw more light on the problem, how the parents might be best advised about their management at home, and finally whether counseling in the school or in a child guidance clinic was available.

I was to use basically the same method when I left private practice to teach pediatric and psychiatric residents from 1947 through 1967, first at the Rochester (Minnesota) Child Health Project, later at the University of Pittsburgh, then at Western Reserve in Cleveland. A teacher or a public-health nurse assigned to a school would ask for a conference on a child with a school problem. I would take a small group of residents to the school, where we'd meet with the teacher and nurse, along with the principal and perhaps the previous year's teacher, for a two-hour conference. The participants found these sessions interesting and valuable. Pediatricians and child psychiatrists who had reached the stage of practice and teaching found this approach—what can be done short of psychotherapy—useful.

I had thought that Andover and Yale, both of which were founded in the eighteenth century, offered the best possible education in America, perhaps the world. In her very kind way, without attacking these institutions I was so proud of, Caroline let me know that educational theory and practice had gone way beyond them. She told me about the principles of progressive education, particularly those of Dewey, whom I had never studied. He had downgraded memory as an aspect of learning and had put the emphasis on learning by doing: and on the project method.

The project method was in contrast to the traditional elementary-school teaching of subjects such as arithmetic, reading, writing, and social studies in isolation from one another. For the project method you would find some broad subject that children of that age are interested in. Caroline Zachry gave the example of Native Americans for the third grade. Kids are fascinated with these people (whom we've always called Indians, sticking to the mistake of the early explorers), perhaps because they choose to wander freely instead of going to the office. In the project method you would read books about Native Americans, you would write about them, you would count the way that they counted. Social studies would include the places where different tribes of Native Americans lived, how and why they traveled in different seasons, what they believed in, and how they organized their tribes. The project method is particularly useful in motivating a child who lacks eagerness to learn for the sake of learning and also one who is significantly behind in one subject such as reading. The child is likely to be stirred by the natural appeal of the subject, and, if he gets involved in one aspect of it—for instance, building a model of a Native American village—this will provide motivation to read about such a village.

The project method immediately made sense to me. Good medical education, where memorization is of limited importance, has always been essentially a project method where you learn by doing, with the patient as the central subject of study. Textbooks and lectures are of some help, but by themselves they will never produce a physician. Physicians have to deal with patients, have to take sensitive histories, must do thoughtful physical examinations, must prescribe laboratory tests with discretion; must put all of these together, consider various possible diagnoses, and discover the most likely one—all under the supervision of teachers.

Since the nineteenth century the first two years of medical education have been dedicated exclusively to the laboratory sciences of anatomy, physiology, chemistry, bacteriology, and pathology. This was logical. But its fault is that it encourages students to forget about their future patients as human beings. It makes them impersonal.

At Western Reserve, beginning in 1955, I participated in a program (already in place), the first of its kind, that represented a further progressive step beyond traditional medical education: *first-year* medical students were each assigned a patient, a pregnant woman in the last trimester of pregnancy. Regularly attending the prenatal clinic with her, the students found that most of the obstetrical residents called these patients (relatively poor women) by their first name. The students considered this somewhat disrespectful; and when they found their patients being treated inconsiderately or rudely by nurses and residents, they were outraged. After all, they had only one patient each and identified strongly with her. Indignant, they would complain to their preceptor, who dealt with them in groups of eight to discuss their experiences with patients. We preceptors had to say to them that we couldn't change the behavior of all the residents in obstetrics, since they weren't under our authority at all but that we could discuss such things, through faculty channels. We also told our students, "It's good for you to see how patients are sometimes mistreated—perhaps that will keep you from becoming insensitive or rude to your future patients." This experience of having responsibility for a patient

*Benjamin Spock, M.D., 1927.*

from the start of medical school and of identifying with her emotionally, had a profound influence in making and keeping our students sensitive—an example of learning by feeling.

It's ironic that all through my childhood and youth I yearned to be a more "regular guy." But in adulthood I turned to new or controversial aspects of pediatrics to cultivate: the psychological aspects of child care, progressive education at every level of schooling, and eventually, political activism to save the world for children.

*Giving Mike a bath at 7 months.*

# 10

I WAS VERY EAGER to have children. Sadly, our first child was born premature. The baby weighed a little over three pounds and died in two days. We didn't give the baby a name, and we gave his body to the medical school. We tried to make as little as possible of his short life, believing at the time that this was the wise and courageous thing to do. Now I think that attitude was wrong in all respects.

This happened while I was being treated at Presbyterian Hospital for spontaneous pneumothorax, assumed in those days to be tuberculous. About two months later, when the doctors thought it was safe for me to travel, our families gave us money to go to Europe. Perhaps the stress of having the baby die together with my having a disease at that time thought to be serious would explain why it was not at all a happy two months that we spent in the south of France. We thought the climate would be like Florida's, but in April and May just a few polar bear types went swimming. For a while I thought I was developing the symptoms of active tuberculosis and was dissatisfied with the checkup I received.

Mike was born in 1933, when I was finishing my psychiatric

residency and had not yet started my psychoanalytic training. Mike was breast-fed, and I gave him bottles from time to time with great pleasure and pride. And I changed his diapers and gave him baths. But I was still under the strong influence of the traditional pediatric teaching that you must be careful not to spoil a child. Mike had periods during his first year when he would wake up and cry at night. I told Jane she shouldn't go to him; it would only encourage him to cry more often and seek company at night. I was old-fashioned all the way. When John was born in 1944, eleven years later—I was knee-deep in writing *Baby and Child Care*, and my ideas in this and many other areas had undergone considerable change.

There is a picture of Mike somewhere between nine and twelve months, being pushed by me in his carriage in Central Park. You can see my immense pride as a father. You can also see how dapper I dressed. I had on a well-fitting overcoat and a Homburg hat at a slightly rakish tilt.

I was one of those fathers who love to give their baby exciting experiences. One of the games I would play with Mike would be to give the baby carriage a push on the sidewalk and run to catch up to it. That would excite Mike and thrill me too. Of course, a thing that appeared to be so foolishly dangerous would distress Jane.

When Mike was three, we entered him in the small private nursery school that was connected, for teaching purposes, with Payne Whitney Clinic's Department of Psychiatry; the residents could observe normal emotional development there. At age five he went to a kindergarten run by a couple who had a very good reputation. The woman was rather managerial. Her husband was considerably older and very much a child at heart. In each of the rooms there was something that you might call a treehouse—a platform raised up from the floor, with lots of appealing places to crawl around and hide in. Mike stayed at this school through first grade.

Now, in this latter school they had used the "look-and-say" reading method, where the student learns to read whole words at a time. For most children this is a quicker way of learning to read than by spelling and sounding out. But it's also a pitfall for ten percent of the pupils, mostly boys, who have dyslexia.

Mike started out first grade with great enthusiasm, but within a month or two he was somewhat tense and unhappy. We didn't know why. A friend of Caroline Zachry's happened to be visiting the school and later told her that a child there had severe dyslexia. Caroline did a little inquiring and found out it was Mike. He was not able to distinguish readily between left and right, the beginning of the word and the end of the word. The words "God" and "dog" looked almost identical to him. We found a tutor for Mike who was a real expert on this particular disability, and that improved things. But we also shifted him to Fieldston School for his second-grade year.

Fieldston School is a progressive, Ethical Culture school in the Bronx. It was a very happy experience for Mike, with I think only two drawbacks. First, it had a lot of very bright, academically fast children, and Mike was aware that he could not compete well with them. But I was happy with the breadth of education. For instance, the children were learning tolerance for children of other backgrounds and from other countries. It made me realize that during those school years there is a natural inclination for children to become cliquish and intolerant of those from a different background. I saw how far a school could go in overcoming this natural developmental tendency to intolerance.

The other trouble with Fieldston School was that it was way up in the Bronx. Not only did Mike have to be picked up by a school bus, but no other children in our neighborhood in New York went there. By not attending a neighborhood school, Mike didn't form any close friendships with children in the neighborhood.

My schedule was getting moderately busy. On weekdays when Mike was in school, I was either at the office or at New York Hospital, and on weekends I was always on call for sick calls. Some smart doctors belong to a group whose members trade off on weekends. But I was not close enough to another pediatrician to do that regularly—just once in a while. Besides, I wanted to take care of my patients in my own way and to be ready to respond to them whenever and however they needed.

When Mike was about eight years old, we started taking in events on Saturday or Sunday such as a museum or a hockey game at Madison Square Garden, with or without Jane as she wished, something that both Mike and I would enjoy. An important aspect of my relationship with Mike was that I wanted to relive my childhood more ideally and more pleasurably through him.

I couldn't convince Jane that I was a dutiful father, partly because when I took Mike out, it was to an event I also wanted to go to. And it certainly was true that whenever an emergency call came I interrupted my family plans, feeling that a doctor must respond first to his patients' needs, and that this took precedence over the family. I think that is a problem with many doctors' families. And it leaves many families resentful.

But I did my best to be very conscientious about my family *and* my patients. If I took Mike to a hockey game, I called the office at intermission to check for messages. If we went out to dinner or to friends' apartments, I always let the exchange know where I was, and if there was any kind of emergency, I would leave. That did not happen very often. I think it's more in adult medicine and internal medicine that doctors get sick calls during the evening, when adults begin to worry about their own symptoms. It's in the latter half of the afternoon that parents discover that children are sick or have a fever, and call. Once children have gone to sleep, even if they have started an illness, they usually stay asleep.

In those days it never occurred to me *not* to make a house visit. All the pediatricians I knew made house visits. Besides, I was under a lot of pressure to make a living at that time. Or, to put it more sharply, I was anxious and embarrassed that I was not making a decent living for my family.

I certainly was not a permissive parent. I'd say without hesitation that I was on the strict side. Later on when Mike and John were

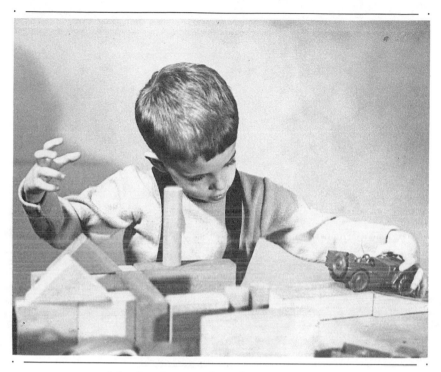

*John Spock at age 5, Rochester, Minnesota.*

adults and were interviewed by reporters to see what the childhood of the sons of the pediatrician who wrote the book was like, both of them always said, "He was a strict father!" I think that they perceived that correctly. I was a strict father in that I had exact and relatively high expectations. Mike says now that he said I was strict to counteract the accusation that I was permissive.

I certainly do not think I was an ideal father by any means! At the Adirondack League Club, where we spent our summers, I built a paddle-wheel boat for Mike. I used empty oilcans for buoyancy and added orange crates and baling wire to make the wheels. It was ingenious, and Mike enjoyed it, but it certainly was too complicated for him at three or four to make himself or to even participate in the making. It was my idea and my execution; that's not ideal in playing with a child.

From early childhood I had wanted toy trains. (It's normal, I

*Mike (16) and John (5), Rochester, Minnesota.*

think, for boys to want to control a miniature form of something that is intriguing in the real world.) I played with Mansfield Horner's trains and assumed that my parents couldn't afford to give them to me. The way I was brought up, I had to kowtow to their decisions without begging.

I bought Mike HO-gauge trains when he was not more than four years old. HO-gauge trains, being very miniature, require a lot of skill both to run and to make the layout—they are more appropriate for a fourteen-year-old boy. I wanted to give Mike anything that I had greatly craved as a child and hadn't gotten, but I couldn't recognize that if you do give your son such intricate toys at the age of four or five, you shouldn't complain or interfere when he is not using them skillfully. I would tell him, "No, no, you don't push it along the floor, you put it on the tracks." And "Wait, we've got to lay down the tracks and we've got to make a layout with switches, sidings, stations." The result of my interference and setting the standards was that Mike lost interest in trains within a few hours. I made the same mistake of being too controlling later with John, and with the same trains and the same result.

When Mike was about three years old, he went through a weepy period. This bothered me a great deal. I would hiss at him, "Don't be a booby!" I'm still ashamed of the intensity of my disapproval and the scorn I used on my own child. The things that I was scornful about were not at all the same things that would provoke my mother. But the technique was the same, as was the intensity of the disapproval.

As far as physical punishment goes, I once gave Mike a sort of

*First grandchild, Dan Spock.*

symbolic swat when he was about fourteen. He had gone on a river trip on a branch of the Colorado River. We had asked him to write us at least a brief note or even a postcard once a week. For eight weeks we never heard a word. At the moment he came home, my impatience welled up, and I gave him a swat on the behind.

I don't remember ever hitting John. I rejected physical punishment on principle and instead used my strong moral disapproval, as my mother had done, but I didn't really approve of that either. One of the things that pushed me to be strict was my anxiety that my sons should not do anything to give themselves or their family a bad reputation. While in some areas I am defiant, as in my politics, I do care about what the neighbors think. When my mother taught us that it's very important whether people like you or not, she wasn't talking about popularity; she was saying that people should not have a basis for disapproving of us on moral grounds. Partly it was sensitivity about my views on child rearing that produced anxiety about my sons' behavior. But it was also because I knew that people enjoy finding that the child of a child specialist, particularly one who has written a book, has problems. They are getting back at the professional who makes them feel inadequate or guilty, and it relieves them of the obligation to take him seriously. For the same reason, people also enjoy a little delinquency in a clergyman's child.

WHEN MIKE WAS BORN in January, 1933, I was in the last part of my psychiatric residency and had not been in pediatric practice at all, so I had hardly begun to think about how to integrate psychological concepts into pediatric advice. With Mike, for instance, I believed in a regular feeding schedule of every four hours, right from birth. By the time I was writing *Baby and Child Care* and John was born in 1944, I believed that it was good to work toward regularity but that there is no need to let the baby cry. On the other hand, just because you hear a whimper in the baby's

Turtle *on Buzzards Bay*.

room does not mean you have to dash in and give him a bottle. This is one of the ways that an experienced parent differs from an inexperienced parent: an inexperienced mother is apt to be so anxious and alert that as soon as she hears the baby stir in his sleep and whimper she hurries in, while the same mother when she has her second or third child will wait a few minutes to see if the baby goes back to sleep again if it's nowhere near four or even three hours since the last feeding.

Child care, both physical and psychological, changed between the time that Mike was born and John was born and between John's birth and the birth of his new twins. My advice to grandparents is still to stay out of it. But if there's something that the parents *want* to know, explain it without being bossy. With parents, and with readers too, I *try* not to cram my ideas down their throats—just to present them with such knowledge as we have about what motivates children at different ages, and let them take over from there. But, for example, with inoculations, parents don't know that from instinct. You have to say what the Academy of Pediatrics recommends. But I try to give the least possible arbitrary advice.

I'm often asked how much control do I think parents should or can have over their kids. Parents have to be responsible for their children, not only their safety but the building of their character. They have to give their children guidance constantly. That includes training them at the age of two, three, and four not to run across the street. Parents have to be very emphatic about not doing things that are dangerous: playing near the stove and playing with matches. On the other hand, I'm a firm believer as a parent that you shouldn't get arbitrary about matters you can't control—for example, insisting that the child is to eat a certain food or disregarding how the child feels about various foods. You shouldn't try to get children to eat more than they are eager for at any meal. How much control you want to exert depends on the area. I think mainly it's a matter of common sense, not a matter of theory. But just having the knowledge isn't enough. Everybody has a strong feeling about how to treat a child. My feelings often made me override what I knew theoretically to be correct.

During my adolescence and youth I resented all sorts of things, but those resentments progressively eased. Partly it was psychoanalysis, but mainly it was the process of maturing in my twenties, as it is for most people, during which time they come to identify with their parents and see that they were doing the best they knew how. Mark Twain once observed, "When I was a boy of fourteen, my father was so ignorant I could hardly stand to have the old man around. But when I got to be twenty-one, I was astonished at how much he had learned in seven years."

*The price is raised to 35 cents.*

# I I

A S I TRIED to develop a pediatric practice, and support my family, there were several factors that made it unusually difficult for me. The most influential was the confusion in the minds of my colleagues—especially the obstetricians who are the source of most pediatric referrals—as to whether I was a pediatrician or a child psychiatrist. I had had a year of psychiatric residency, five years of part-time psychoanalytical training, several evening seminars, and two years of analysis. All this training was supposed to help me give psychologically correct advice to mothers, and despite my colleagues' confusion, I considered myself first and foremost a pediatrician.

Another factor, of course, was that I started in at the bottom of the Depression, the year that the banks were closed. Even experienced, distinguished pediatricians were not as busy as they had been. The head of pediatrics at New York Hospital said casually one day that he had plenty of time to sit and read journals, and I was relieved to hear that I was not the only pediatrician with too little to do. Couples were postponing having children, and those who already had them found they could survive without routine checkups.

Most important was the fact that there was no obstetrician who particularly valued my combined training and referred patients steadily to me. The obstetrician who delivered Mike and our premature baby had told me during both of Jane's pregnancies that he couldn't wait for me to get into pediatric practice, so that he could start referring patients to me. I thought this would guarantee my success because, after all, he was a very successful obstetrician in private practice as well as being head of the department at Columbia. But he was also an absent-minded person and after I actually started my practice, he failed to refer any patients to me for five or six years, and then his first and only referral was a fifteen-year-old girl with a full-blown paranoid-schizophrenia, who belonged in a psychiatric hospital.

During the ten years between the time I started my practice and wrote *Baby and Child Care*, I was trying to take the psychoanalytic concepts I was studying and somehow fit them together with what mothers were telling me about their babies. My psychoanalytic training told me, for example, that when parents go at toilet training too early and too harshly, the baby may rebel, and if prolonged it may contribute to a somewhat compulsive personality makeup. But when I asked my psychoanalytic mentors and my fellow students at the New York Psychoanalytic Institute how they would suggest parents go about toilet training, they shrugged their shoulders because none of them had had that kind of experience. With their adult patients they were working with impressions left over in the unconscious minds from early childhood, but they had no experience at turning this into positive, practical advice for parents.

During most of those first ten years, I really suffered and sweated trying to figure out the best advice I could give. And then I was always waiting eagerly to ask the mother how it worked out.

One of my officemates said to me one day in great perplexity, "Ben, why do you care about thumb-sucking?"—it wasn't a tra-

ditional pediatric concern, even though all mothers ask their pediatrician how to prevent it or cure it. It was a very good example
of how I differed from most pediatricians. To exaggerate, their
greatest interest was looking for an "interesting" case, an example
of a relatively rare disease that would call on their skills in diagnosis
and treatment. The rare "interesting" case never happened to interest me. For some reason, I always wanted to know about *everyday* things, like finding ways of preventing colds or, more
importantly, a way of abbreviating a cold after a child catches it (I
used to emphasize keeping the child evenly warm because of my
experience with my own colds.) Probably I was interested in the
common psychological problems because those were the things
parents were interested in and I identified with them in trying to
find the answers.

My practice was small by any standards and grew slowly. This
at least allowed me and the parents of my patients the luxury of
two-hour first visits and half-hour return visits, though there were
telephone interruptions of course. Without meaning to do this
intentionally, I encouraged telephone abuse by discussing any
problem at length, even when I was with another patient. One
amiable but rather humorless mother whose appointment had been
interrupted continuously for an entire hour by a succession of such
calls was never able to get my answer to the one big question she'd
come to ask and finally said without a trace of sarcasm, "I see how
busy you are today. I'll just call you on the phone sometime!"

My practice was weighted with families who wanted their pediatric care to be psychologically sound; the parents were dispro-
portionately psychoanalysts, psychologists, social workers, and
people who had been analyzed themselves.


A FTER I HAD BEEN IN PRACTICE for only five years, an editor
from Doubleday came to ask me to write a book for parents.
I was completely unknown, but a publisher in New York inquiring
around among professors of pediatrics might have stumbled on me

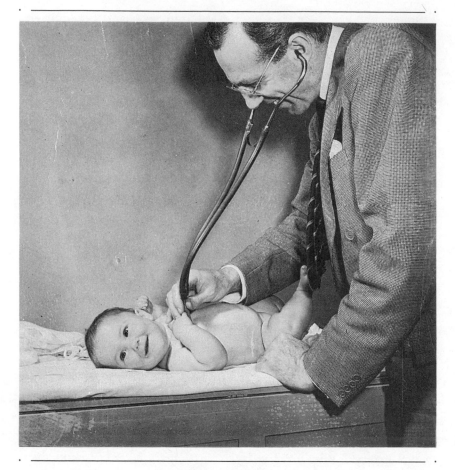

*Doctor at work.*

as a doctor who had psychological as well as pediatric training. Immediately I told Doubleday that I didn't know enough. I wasn't tempted in the slightest, because I was having enough trouble finding out what to tell my own patients, let alone ten thousand other people through a book. Doubleday went away, and another five years went by before an editor from Pocket Books came, a droll fellow named Donald Geddes, who told me, The book we want doesn't really have to be very good, because we are only going to charge a quarter and can sell ten thousand copies a year easily!

Putting it that way, though he was really only joking, made it easier for me to accept. First of all, ten thousand copies a year meant reaching a lot of people. That appealed to the do-gooder in me. And his saying that it didn't have to be very good, this relieved me of the need to be perfect in my advice. I agreed to try. So it had taken me ten years to learn enough—from mothers and babies—to feel comfortable about my advice. It was mothers and babies who contributed the substance of the book.

People ask how I knew I could write a book. Spocks of my generation never doubted that they could write. Anytime we were away from home for a week or more, for boarding school, for summer camp, or for college, we had to write my mother twice a week and tell her in detail what we had been doing every morning, afternoon, and evening, who with, and what kind of people they were. She was possessive, and also fearful that we'd somehow fall in with evil companions. Once at Andover when I had let more than four days go by without writing, she sent me a telegram saying, "Write or come home," and I didn't doubt that she meant it.

People also ask whether I did a lot of library research or went over all my patient records to write the book. I did none of either. That ten years of practice was one long, elaborate experiment. Every time a mother told me something even slightly different from my previous concepts, I revised my ideas accordingly. What went into the manuscript each day was my latest conclusion on that subject, the end result of numberless revisions. At that point it was as simple as reading a computer printout.

I did crib two ideas from recent books. One, by a casual New York pediatrician named Bartlett, had been dictated to a smart mother in answer to her questions, so it came out in a chatty style that was comforting to mothers. I also noted that Gesell and Ilg's first book reassured and delighted parents because they found that their baby's development was within normal limits. I resolved to give not the earliest or the average age for each step but the slowest that was normal.

Interviewers often ask me as well to state my "theories" of child-raising. I never set out to impose any such grand design on the parents of the world. In fact, it grew increasingly clear to me as I continued to practice that there were *so many* experts, with the best of intentions, telling parents what to do—that parents' most widespread problem was their own uncertainty, a guilty feeling of "Maybe I don't know enough . . . maybe I need to read another book!" Less secure parents begin to think that only professionals know the answers. They don't dare trust their own judgment or stand firm. It's pathetic, and children can get pesky when they sense their parents' uncertainty.

This was so different from my own mother who, like so many of her generation, never had a moment's doubt—wouldn't even listen to a child's plea or statement. She *knew* what was good for health and morals, and you'd better not irritate her by raising questions. The change began, I believe, in the first part of the twentieth century, with a psychologist named John Watson who advocated never kissing or comforting your child, for fear of spoiling him. You could shake hands with him. If you wanted him to grow up to be a musician, you played music to him from infancy. Watson's mechanical view of psychology and his absolutism jolted parents and impressed quite a few. Henry Holt, the pediatrician and author, was dictatorial about healthy foods, and people like my mother responded to him with absolute reverence.

Increasing masses of information about diet, health, and behavior came flooding out. Much of the information filled a need, but the effect on the less self-assured parents was to unsettle them and undermine their natural impulses and their self-confidence.

This reliance on distant experts was fostered by the increasing mobility of young families and the fragmentation of the extended family. The awe-inspiring expert took the place of the reassuring grandmother.

Yet another factor that seriously shook sensitive parents was the new, oversimplified notion that when there were behavior disturbances in children, it was always the result of parents' mistakes in handling them. This idea didn't exist in earlier centuries, but was propagated in the first three decades of this one by those who were mobilizing up support for the mental hygiene and child guidance clinic movements. It was a case of opening Pandora's box.

My purpose was not to advocate a theory, but primarily to tell parents what children are like, including descriptions of their unconscious drives. This was a big change from earlier manuals, with their stern dictums. I was just trying to show confidence in parents and to reassure them whenever possible. I certainly never advocated a permissive philosophy. I have always believed that parents should respect their children but also ask for respect from them, too. It was certainly not my principal aim to give them a whole bookful of "do's" and "don'ts."

B*ABY AND CHILD CARE* sold three-quarters of a million copies the first year without advertising or promotion, just word-of-mouth recommendations. I think the reasons were that it was cheap, it was complete, and it dealt with both the psychological and the physical sides of child care. But most important by far was that I wrote the book with the resolve not to scare parents, or boss them around, or talk down to them. The most rewarding fan letters I got said simply, "It sounds as if you're talking to me as if you think I'm a sensible person."

The very first sentence of *Baby and Child Care* reads: "Trust yourself. You know more than you think you do." I put this in as a token of my respect for parents, but I didn't really expect it to have much impact. Yet everywhere I go, I hear that first sentence quoted with approval—and that pleases me.

Since *Baby and Child Care* gave parents a lot more information and advice than any previous book had done—much of it newfangled—I was watching anxiously for reviews and comments from the medical profession, especially pediatricians. The first review came in the *Journal of the American Medical Association*, and it said in effect that it was a pretty good book with sensible advice. Its only criticism was that too often it repeats the phrase "Consult your own doctor." It couldn't have said anything that would re-

*Ben the New Yorker, early 1960s.*

assure *me* more! Nobody could criticize me for by-passing the physician—the *JAMA* says I'm leaning over too far backward.

Needless to say, I was also nervous about what my mother would think of *Baby and Child Care*. When a young man writes a book about how to raise children, in a sense it's his reflection on the way his mother raised him. I sent a copy to my mother, of course. The first time she came down to New York, she said, "Benny, I think it's quite sensible." That astounded me, because it deviated

so far from her convictions about such matters as sex and masturbation, but I accepted her review with gratitude.

There was no advertising for *Baby and Child Care*. The book
was sold by word of mouth. After it had been out awhile, Charlie
Duell of Duell Sloan and Pearce, the hardcover publisher, pro-
posed an advertisement or two, which I thought were atrocious.
One of them was a cartoon with a scream in a balloon coming out
of the baby's room and the mother looking terrified, and the word-
ing was: "When the baby screams in the middle of the night, how
do you know what it means?" Well, I tried to tell Charlie, "My
God, the whole idea of the book is not to scare parents but to
reassure them—this is totally out of character."

One of the first television shows to mention my book was *I Love
Lucy*. It was in 1953 at the time when Lucy and Desi were having
a baby in actuality (their second, but their first as a character on
the show) and were incorporating their questions and arguments
about the baby into the show. When they discussed what to do
about the baby, they repeatedly concluded, "Well, let's see what
Spock says." They never sneered at the book's advice. I always
credit them with helping greatly to popularize the book.

NOWADAYS when they come and ask you to write a book, they
pay you an advance. They didn't offer me one, and if they
had, I would have turned it down, saying I'd rather have the
royalties spread as the book earns money.

I had two big fights with Pocket Books. One was my persistent
request for a higher royalty rate. For a number of years I made
only about five thousand dollars a year on the book, though it was
selling at a phenomenal rate. I protested on the basis that they
didn't have to pay half their royalties to a hardcover publisher, the
usual arrangement between an original hardcover publisher and a
paperback reprinter, since they, Pocket Books, had originated the
book themselves. That was a perfectly rational basis for pleading
with them. However, there was no legal basis for it and they

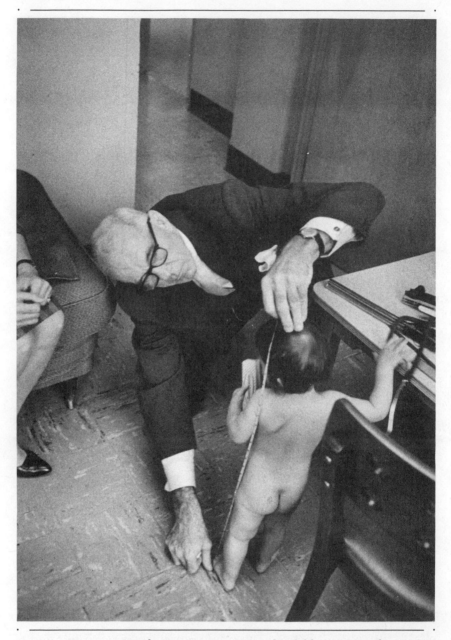

*Examining Linda Diener, a patient in the child-rearing study
at Western Reserve.*

wouldn't agree—until they wanted me to write two other books, and I said I'd write them if they would double the royalties on *Baby and Child Care*, which they did.

My second fight was to get the advertising out of *Baby and Child Care*. At one point, Pocket Books got the idea of putting advertising into many of their paperbacks, cookbooks for instance, where they thought it would be appropriate. They were particularly hot to put advertisements in *Baby and Child Care* because its sales were tremendous and there were many products—baby food, baby clothes, diapers, lotions—that would be eager to advertise. I protested but, in retrospect, not vigorously enough. I should have raised hell, I should have said, "Over my dead body, I'll fight you in the courts and I'll fight you on television!" They even tried to buy my agreement by offering to share the advertising proceeds with me. But I said I didn't want to get involved by taking money for advertising. Anyway, they put advertising in. I did have some control: I got the right to veto any advertisement I thought was undignified or not factual, like the one that so many medical products use, "Doctors recommend . . ."

After I protested repeatedly for a number of years, I tried at one point to start a suit against them but found that they could drag the case out forever. However, they wanted me to write another book, one for teenagers about sex, and said if I would do this they would take the advertising out of *Baby and Child Care*. So I wrote *A Teenager's Guide to Life and Love*. I made it as sound, spiritually as well as medically, as I knew how. Well, it had only a modest success. It was much too conservative. I had thought that young people had gotten as casual about sex as they would ever get, and I saw my book as coinciding with a move back to a more traditional emphasis on the spiritual side of sexuality and on chastity. But I was totally wrong. Sexuality continued to be liberalized, if that's the right word. But the publisher had to take out the advertising and never put it back in.

. . .

B*ABY AND CHILD CARE* was an instant success—far more than I
or Pocket Books had ever anticipated—but fame came gradually. For instance, when I would go to a motel in my travels and
the operator would ask my name when I was leaving my wakeup
call, I would say, "Benjamin Spock." For the first six or eight years
after the book came out, I got no recognition from hotel/motel
operators. But then occasionally an operator would say, "Oh, just
like the Doctor!"

Fifteen years after the book's publication, I got an honorary
degree from Durham University, in England. The vice-chancellor's
wife was a boarding school roommate of Jane's, which I'm sure
played the largest part in my selection, but I was honored all the
same. What made this one particularly exciting for me was that
Charlie Chaplin, the Royal Ballet choreographer Frederick Ashton,
and the poet W. H. Auden also received degrees. That's fancy
company!

Durham has the oldest Gothic cathedral in England, dating from
the late eleventh century. It's a huge, imposing, edifice that shares
a citadel in the middle of Durham with a castle from the same
period. Our robes for the honorary degrees were really impressive:
scarlet wool for the main part of the robe and scarlet satin on the
facings. The caps were not the usual mortarboards of most American
universities, but black velvet cushions.

While we waited for the ceremony to begin, Charlie Chaplin
was telling stories to the chancellor, who was thrice a lord: by birth,
by being chancellor of the university (a purely honorary position),
and by his office of lord chamberlain to the Queen. That is to say,
the person who takes care of the Queen's worldly affairs, her accounts, the administration of her estates. So he was, as you can
imagine, excessively conservative in appearance and manner. Charlie Chaplin was spinning one amusing tale after another, and when
he came to the punch line, the chancellor would give a quick little
smirk without any sign of real appreciation or humor. Charlie was
not bothered by this; he would launch into another story, and at
the end the chancellor would give his quick little smirk again.

*Charlie Chaplin, Ben, and two officials of Durham University.*

Finally it was time to go to the main hall of the castle, where the degrees were to be given. Each of us was taken by the elbow and ushered up to the chancellor to receive the degree. As Jane later told me, I instinctively reacted against this implication of dependency by yanking my elbow away.

After the degrees were given, the procession went across the top of the citadel from the castle to the cathedral. I happened to be in line behind Charlie. He came originally from the north of England and he was particularly loved there, so when the towns-people, who were thronging both sides of the line of march, caught sight of him, they grabbed each other and pointed with delight and shouted, "Charlie! Charlie!" And they gave tight little waves—not the flappy waves that we usually give here but a half-fist with a wiggling of the fingers. In this short march, not more than two

city blocks, Charlie himself started out very reserved: he acknowl-
edged this applause with a nod of his head. Then he raised his
hand close to his shoulder and started waving back with that tight
little flutter. Eventually he got caught up in their enthusiasm and
his hand really got circulating as he returned the townspeople's
affection.

We filed into the cathedral. It was enough to give a person
gooseflesh to hear the pealing organ and the singing of the choir.

Afterward there was a reception for the parents of the students
and for friends of the recipients of honorary degrees. One of the
university functionaries who was escorting us around said, "For
this reception, you know, you can take off your robes." Here was
the one chance in our lives to wear scarlet robes and black velvet
cushion caps, and we didn't want it to be over quite so soon! Charlie
Chaplin and I, who were standing close together, both blurted out,
"Do we have to?"

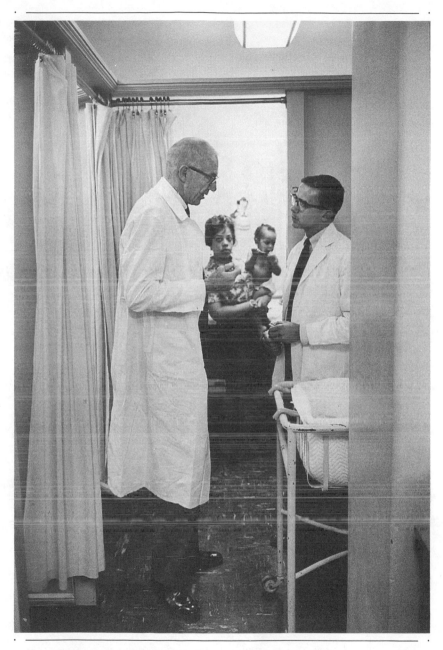

*Doctor as teacher.*

*Lt. Cmdr. Benjamin Spock, M.D., U.S. Navy, 1944.*

# 12

AROUND 1939 OR 1940, when it looked inevitable that the United States would be drawn into World War II, my analyst, Sandor Rado, asked me why I wasn't agitated about the United States's approaching involvement. And I said, quite honestly, "My greatest anxiety was during the Spanish Civil War, because I saw it as a preliminary to World War II. That Hitler would have to be stopped sooner or later."

The Spanish Civil War was horrifying. On the one side, under Franco, were the forces of reaction that got together and eventually overthrew the democratic government of Spain. most of the hierarchy of the Catholic Church, the army, and the industrialists. And the governments of the United States and Great Britain and France—which should have been on the side of the elected government of Spain—hypocritically stated that they believed in noninterference. Which meant, in practice, allowing Fascist Italy and Germany under Hitler to aid Franco and help overthrow the democracy. When Franco won out, I saw World War II as inevitable.

I was more churned up, more anxious, more despairing, about what happened in Spain than at any other period. I would jump out of bed in the morning and rush to get the *New York Times* at the apartment door to find out what was happening. But it never occurred to me to become an activist in the sense of going to Spain. I could have enlisted in the Abraham Lincoln Brigade as a physician.

I WAS IN PRACTICE in New York City on December 7, 1941, when the Japanese attack on Pearl Harbor brought America into World War II. Jane had taken Mike to see *Dumbo* that Sunday afternoon when I heard of the attack. When they came home I said, "The Japanese have attacked Pearl Harbor." Jane said, "The movie was wonderful, you should have gone." I had to repeat what I'd said; this time she appreciated its enormous significance. Soon our government began calling up all physicians for physical examinations. Doctors in World War II were drafted almost like ordinary young citizens. They were offered a commission, and if they refused it, the government just drafted them as privates.

I had a history of spontaneous pneumothorax back in 1931 when that condition was considered probably tuberculosis. And shortly before I was called up for examination, I had had viral pneumonia. They took an X-ray, which showed a lobe of one of my lungs to be consolidated. That scared them off; they said, "We can't use you." It was a practical matter for the government: if they take a person in and he turns out to have a disease, they owe him a pension for the rest of his life. As a pediatrician I was willing but not eager to participate, and I had a legitimate medical excuse. I was busier than ever before, because they were taking doctors out of private practice fairly rapidly. It was exciting to be really busy at last. Two years after I was turned down I agreed to write *Baby and Child Care* and Jane and I decided to have a baby, both on the assumption that I was turned down for good—they'd been so emphatic about it.

We had moved from Park Avenue at 95th Street to a more modest apartment on 90th Street because the rent was going up and we saw that the future was uncertain. In 1944 I got a second call to come for a physical examination. I assumed that as soon as they heard that I had had a consolidated lung in 1942 and a spontaneous pneumothorax in 1931, they would turn me down again. I casually asked the medical captain in charge what he thought the chances were, and he said, "I think there's every chance that you'll be taken." I was really surprised and upset—Jane even more so.

I got in touch with Randy Bailey, a former fellow intern and my personal physician, who was by this time in the Navy in Washington, working on the assignment of doctors. IIe thought a physician would be much more likely to be assigned to his own line of work in the Navy than in the Army because it was much smaller and could be a little more careful. So I told the proper authorities that I would like to be in the Navy, and they began processing my request for a commission as a lieutenant commander. I was told to report for a two-month orientation to Bethesda Naval Medical Center (every medical institution with any pride is now a "center," even an animal hospital). When my son, Mike, at age 11 heard that I was going into the Navy, he was unhappy. He said he didn't want me to be buried at sea. He was taking a grim view of the whole situation.

I was uneasy on the train to Washington, wearing my uniform for the first time. I felt like an impostor. My instructions said that if I came upon sailors making a disturbance, I was to take charge. I had no idea how to curb a dozen drunken sailors.

Coming into the Navy as I had straight out of private practice, where for the last months I'd been too busy to dare lose a minute, suddenly being faced with the slow pace of orientation was dislocating and stressful, like screeching to a halt. They wanted to use me as a psychiatrist, which was logical, since they didn't need many pediatricians. So I was assigned to the psychiatric department along with half a dozen other doctors new to the Navy. Our instructions were to appear every morning at eight and wait for an assignment from the commander in charge. He was a sourpuss regular Navy psychiatrist who had his own administrative work to do. So it was usually not until nine or ten that he got around to assigning us. Our job would be to take a psychiatric history and do physical and psychiatric examinations on a recently admitted patient.

A couple of weeks into my stay at Bethesda, I went to a dance at a country club for the hospital staff. About midnight a call came through from New York. Jane was in labor. There were no more planes or trains that night, but I was on hand for the first plane, at 7:00 A.M. At New York Hospital I found that Jane's labor had stopped when she got the message that I couldn't get there that night. But it started up again when I appeared, and John was soon born.

Every weekend when I went back to New York, though delighted to see my family, I was slightly grumpy and uncommunicative. Other officers, I found, were having the same experience. I remembered the same disappointment, a very slight depression, on coming home from Andover for a vacation that I had been looking forward to for months. In that case it seemed clear that I had felt more grown-up by having been away from the family for months, meeting new challenges, changing into a different person. And when I came back to New York from Bethesda, it was as if I were being treated no differently than when I'd first left home.

The same thing happened when I was discharged from the Navy. After two years of service I was eager to go home. But once there, I found myself again grumpy and uncommunicative. Some others I knew went into a real depression. I felt that I had become a different person and should be treated differently when I returned home. It was also the euphoria of getting out of the service: nothing can be as good as what you've dreamed about.

AFTER I'D BEEN two months in Bethesda, Randy Bailey got me assigned to the U.S. Naval Hospital, St. Alban's, in Queens, New York. Now I could live with my family in Manhattan. The hospital was a huge compound filled with rows and rows of temporary one-story structures. I walked miles to get from my ward to the hospital office.

My ward, number 134, was a locked disciplinary psychiatric ward where they put sailors who had proved to be irresponsible psychopaths (now called sociopaths) and who had committed a number of increasing offenses—mostly "absent over leave." The ward was locked because these sailors were prisoners.

Neglected in childhood, they had developed defective personalities, being very demanding and impulsive and having very little sense of responsibility.

I was to take histories on these patients and get them suitably diagnosed and discharged from the Navy. I had to write them up correctly so that when the papers went to Washington for review, the diagnosis would be recognized as suitable. We didn't try to give them any therapy; to successfully treat such characters would take years. Our main job, meanwhile, was to keep peace in the ward while these restless irresponsibles waited for their discharge.

I tried to keep morale up with the staff. Every morning I had a staff meeting with the corpsmen and nurses. If there had been a new patient admitted in the last twenty-four hours, one of the corpsmen would have taken the history, I would have confirmed it, and he would present it at the staff meeting. The Navy was trying to give these maladapted people a discharge that wouldn't entitle them to a pension for the rest of their lives. Anybody with a *medical* discharge, even if it was only a ten-percent disability, got a pension. So, instead of being called psychopaths, they were labeled "inapt for naval service," which meant only that they couldn't adjust to the Navy. (The newer term "sociopath" refers to mild character defects such as my irresponsibles had, and also the ineffectuals. "Psychopath" is still the label for people with more severely defective characters, such as criminals.)

Psychopaths and sociopaths are difficult people to live or work with. They are greedy and demanding, and often they are rude. In the Navy they were always impatient to get their papers back.

When I'd make morning rounds, every one of them would demand at least once a week, "Doc, where are my papers? Why haven't my papers come back from Washington?" They were never satisfied with their discharges, which were not dishonorable but not honorable either. I'd answer, "Jenkins, in the olden days they shot deserters. You ought to be grateful." He'd say indignantly, "I know lots of guys who were over the hill longer than I was, and they got better discharges than this!"

Our locked ward had an enclosed courtyard. I got table tennis and volleyball equipment so that there would be something for the patients to do. But a lot of them, instead of using this equipment, would just lie around in their sacks during the day and snooze. Then at night they would be wide awake, looking for mischief.

Occasionally a mentally retarded person would turn up on our ward for repeated offenses; yet every draftee had been given a mental test. I finally solved the puzzle. A kindly petty officer would give the mental test to a whole roomful of draftees. If a man was struggling and couldn't find the answers to these questions, the petty officer would take mercy on him and help him find the right answer. This was poor judgment, because it would end up costing thousands of dollars, first, to get this man into the Navy, give him his orientation and training, give him his uniform and his shoes, feed him, try him and keep him in the brig, and keep him in the hospital for a month while he was being diagnosed and his papers were being processed in Washington. To do all this, the Navy had to use multiple personnel: Marines to man the brig, doctors, nurses, and corpsmen.

The corpsmen were the first line of contact with these patients. Every time a patient had to go somewhere for a test or for an X-ray or to the office to look into his papers he had to have a corpsman along because he was a prisoner. These patients all had offenses, and most of them were deserters which meant absent for thirty days or more. At night the staff would be cut way down, and that is why these guys tended to get disorderly. They would tease a schizophrenic or feeble-minded patient who would occasionally get on my ward by mistake, rig up his bed so it would fall down with a terrible crash, terrifying the patient and making the rest of the gang hilarious.

In the Navy every ship or every activity like a hospital has a commanding officer and under him an executive officer, who deals with all disciplinary cases. Since all of my patients were disciplinary cases, I had a great deal of contact with the hospital's executive officer, a captain, a stuffy, standoffish sort of person. I once consulted with him when I had a particularly unruly bunch who rioted all night. He said, "Well, all you have to do is make out a written complaint with the help of a corpsman stating exactly what happened at exactly what hour." So I did that after one of these night riots and then sent the culprits down to the "captain's mast," which is the lowest, most informal court in the Navy (not the same as a court-martial). It's for people who have behaved improperly in the last twenty-four hours. The executive officer determines whether the guy is guilty or not, and how guilty, and then assigns some kind of penalty or decides that he should be court-martialed.

In the case of my rioting gang, the ringleaders complained bitterly to the executive officer that the night corpsman was mistreating them. (One night corpsman against a couple of dozen rioters!) The captain sent them back without any punishment at all, and they returned triumphant, laughing uproariously that they had turned the tables. I was indignant. I had gone through all the paperwork to get these men disciplined, and the captain believed them, not me!

After a year at St. Albans I was assigned for a couple of months to Lion Nine, a naval-base hospital that was being assembled and trained to go into the Pacific to participate in the invasion of Japan. It was temporarily located farther out on Long Island at Long Beach. People were trained there for beach landing. They would leap out of boats into the water and rush up the beach. Psychiatrists were always excused from exercises such as this because at every station there was a backlog of cases, mostly the irresponsibles and the complainers. The latter, also known as "sad sacks" or "nervous in the service," were the ones who turned up day after day at sick call, complaining of stomachaches, headaches, backaches, constipation. Medical investigation would reveal no definite physical explanation.

The military services were still demanding more doctors and, at this stage of the war, were scraping the bottom of the barrel. One physician at Long Beach had been promised, at the time he was commissioned, special assignments without physical exertion because of a recent coronary attack. But the promise must have been lost in the shuffle, because he was having to leap into the surf and rush up the beach with the rest, and he was scared.

The Navy assembled Lion Nine at Long Beach, then sent the whole kit and caboodle by troop train to South San Francisco and from there trucked us over to the U.S. Naval Personnel Depot at San Bruno, located in a former racetrack. For several months, until the war ended, that was my permanent assignment, but I was given temporary additional duty in psychiatry at Treasure Island in San Francisco Bay. After that I was assigned to Family Hospital and Clinic at the huge, imposing naval air station in Coronado, outside San Diego. Then I was detached and sent back up the coast to San Leandro, a large naval hospital close to Oak Knoll Hospital, which was the permanent Navy hospital in Oakland. I was discharged from San Leandro in 1946, two years from the time I'd got into the Navy. I was working on *Baby and Child Care* in the evenings the whole time from 1943 to 1946. I did approximately a year of writing before I went into the Navy and another year while at St. Albans. On the troop train to California and in San Bruno I was still doing the index. My job was constantly frustrated by the superannuated warrant officer who shared my Pullman section. He went to sleep after every meal, and his snoring, which started gently and escalated into the loud sounds of strangulation, made indexing utterly impossible.

•  •  •

AT TREASURE ISLAND I had women patients for the first and only time. Waves reacted differently to discharge than the irresponsible males, who couldn't wait to get out. When I would tell them that I was recommending them for discharge, they would burst into tears and say that they didn't want to get out of the Navy. Most of the ones I saw were country girls who had wanted to get away from home but couldn't in peacetime because they had no jobs to go to.

Every one of my duty stations had a backlog of "inapt" sailors to be written up and discharged. I never had the excitement of leaping into the surf and charging up a beach. Or a leisurely life either. The Navy had plenty of surgeons, for instance, but since there was little surgery to do, except after a battle, surgeons could relax, read books or play golf if there was a course nearby. Even after they were sent out into the Pacific there might be nothing to do. Psychiatrists, though, always had work, mostly the same old irresponsibles and sad sacks. But I never did practice any other kind of psychiatry.

There was no psychiatric treatment except for Marines who developed combat fatigue from prolonged combat in such areas as Guadalcanal or Iwo Jima. Lots of physicians were turned into psychiatrists by the Navy. These "thirty-day wonders" were sent to Bethesda to learn how to write up a survey, as the discharge papers were technically called. They needed only enough psychiatric training to be able to make a diagnosis of inapt for naval service and to write up a history and a description that would suit the diagnosis and get the person out of the Navy.

I had a very different experience at Family Hospital and Clinic in Coronado. There I was a pediatrician for the only time in the Navy. I wrote in *Baby and Child Care* that a woman could breast-feed her baby if she wanted to and the staff supported her. But I didn't know for sure whether it was true, because in New York I'd had few patients who wanted to breast-feed and few nurses who were sympathetic. Private patients always stayed in the hospital twelve days at that time. That was enough to ruin almost any attempt to breast-feed, because the baby would only be brought to the mother on a rigid four-hour schedule, omitting the 2:00 A.M. feeding. Most nurses were not sympathetic with the baby or the mother, and most obstetricians were not sympathetic with the mother. I'd had patients in private practice who wanted to breast-feed, but the obstetrician would make remarks like "What do you want to do *that* for?"

Family Hospital and Clinic was essentially an obstetrical hospital for the large number of wives at the air station. I was the only pediatrician, and I was in charge of the nursery. It was exciting and educational to be able to set policy in the nursery. I could say that the babies were to be brought to the mothers when the babies were hungry and that all the babies were to be brought to the mothers at 2:00 A.M. As a pediatrician in New York I could never make such policy decisions. For example, if a mother had a baby at some hospital in New York and told the obstetrician that she wanted me to take care of her baby, the obstetrician would often wait until mother and baby were within a day or two of going home to notify me. The best opportunity for fostering breast-feeding would have passed. And I had no authority—it wasn't my hospital. I would have to ask the head nursery nurse, "Can I put this baby on a three-hour schedule?" and she would say, "No, we only have a four-hour schedule here," or, "We don't wake the mothers at 2:00 A.M." In California I was the doctor in charge of the nursery and I could give orders. We turned out the babies about eighty percent breast-fed.

I also worked in the pediatric outpatient department of Family Clinic, where there were all kinds of children's illnesses. I was interested to see that in California, where a lot of kids went barefoot, they had much better ankles and feet than the children in New York, who by the age of one year are wearing shoes and socks and walking on carpeted floors. I had always guessed that under natural conditions the grass tickles the soles of the foot, making the child arch his foot away from the grass, and that this is what strengthens all the muscles to make a good arch and ankle. I also saw that many children had chronic colds, even though they spent a lot of time outdoors. I speculated that the variable weather, warm at midday and then cold by mid-afternoon, chilled children and tended to keep colds going.

It was fun being in a permanent installation at the naval air station instead of in flimsy temporary buildings. Marine guards saluted us as we drove through the gate. There were two fine swimming pools and two restaurants for officers. The chicken dinner was a dollar fifty, the steak dinner two dollars. Drinks were only fifty cents because there was no tax. There was a dance every Saturday night. Such privileges helped to stretch my five-thousand-dollar lieutenant commander's salary (there was a fairly generous housing allowance too) and to give us the feeling of living in some degree of luxury. Huge aircraft carriers lay at the docks, and military planes darted in and out.

I WAS IN THE NAVY in California waiting to be sent to the invasion of Japan when the bomb was dropped on Hiroshima. Our government was hoping to intimidate the Japanese, including the emperor and to impress the Soviets. When they first announced it, they didn't say it was an atom bomb. I knew that it had caused more destruction than any previous explosion, but I was not aware to what extent.

At the time, I thought it was great to have the war ended unexpectedly early so that we didn't have to get involved in the invasion of Japan, which would have been long and bloody. I took it for granted that dropping the atom bomb had been the wise thing to do. I certainly don't think so now, since we've learned that the Japanese government was considering surrender already.

In the aftermath of World War II there was a period of harsh reaction led by the House Un-American Activities Committee (HUAC), the FBI, Senator Joe McCarthy, and the reactionary press, supported by a majority in Congress and the population.

They were out to get people they accused of being communist sympathizers or even just determined liberals. It was horrifying the way they hounded people for years, many of whom had no verifiable connection or sympathy; they merely had political views different from their accusers. They would be accused publicly before there was any testimony. Later they would be forced to testify not only on what they themselves had been doing politically—HUAC would demand to know who their friends and associates were. If the person being questioned said, "I won't tell who my friends and associates were," they would be prosecuted for contempt of Congress and sent to jail. A lot of people were named and lost their jobs—in the government, in universities, and elsewhere, without an opportunity to defend themselves.

I was never vehemently anticommunist, I was never procommunist, but I thought that the American hysteria about communism was unfounded and harmful to our foreign and domestic policies. I was also opposed to the unconstitutional way that HUAC, the Senate Internal Security Committee, Hoover, and the FBI went about it.

When Hoover died in May 1972, I was asked by the press whether I had any comment. I said it was a relief to have this man silenced who had no understanding of the underlying philosophy of our government or of our Bill of Rights, a man who had such enormous power and used it to harass individuals with whom he disagreed politically, and who had done as much as anyone to intimidate millions of Americans out of their right to hear and judge for themselves all political opinions. Afterward I heard that of the hundreds of comments the press got, mine was the only one that was frankly exuberant.

*The official Navy portrait.*

*Kenny Diener, a patient in the child-rearing study.*

# 13

IN 1956 I WAS ASKED to do a brief television commercial for Stevenson. He was the first presidential candidate I publicly supported. The person who raised the money said they would just like me to be known as supporting Stevenson, and he left it to me what issue to take up. I chose federal aid to education.

In the 1952 campaign Eisenhower had come out for federal aid to education, but when the time came and the bill was hanging in the balance in Congress, when a word from him might have made the difference between nonpassage and passage, he refrained from saying anything and the bill was lost. Yet in 1956 he again said he was for federal aid. This demonstration of insincerity had angered me, so in the commercial I pointed it out and said I supported Stevenson in large part because I believed that he, unlike Eisenhower, would stand firm on this issue.

A batch of hostile letters came, mostly from women, of this general tenor: "How dare you say that? Eisenhower would fight and die for children," so it really shocked me that these people could deny the realities and scold me for being angry at Eisenhower. I was writing a monthly column for the *Ladies' Home Jour-*

*nal* at the time, and I was so upset by these letters that I asked the editor, Mr. Gould, if it would be appropriate for me to explain this view some place in the *Ladies' Home Journal.* He was very amiable, as always, and said I could use the letters-to-the-editor column. And then he added, in his gentle, avuncular manner, "You know, if you stick your neck out into politics, you can expect to get hurt." I thought that over and decided it was very good advice.

IN SEPTEMBER 1960 I announced, in reply to a reporter's question, that I was supporting John Kennedy for the presidency. I felt at that time that I was pretty daring to do that, because a lot of people, including a lot of liberals, thought you can't vote for a Catholic for president, he'd be too much under the sway of the pope. I thought that what he said about having an individual conscience and feeling that he would not be bound by the position of anybody else in the Church was enough of a statement that he would not slavishly follow the Church hierarchy. Well, my endorsement was reported in the press, somebody told Mrs. Kennedy, "I see Dr. Spock has announced he's for your husband," and Mrs. Kennedy replied, "Well, I'm for Dr. Spock." Next thing I knew, I was invited by the Democratic National Committee to come to the Kennedys' home in Georgetown to make a political commercial with Mrs. Kennedy.

It was a beautiful house, but that day it was absolutely full of television equipment. Large cables were strewn all over the floor, a television camera was in the middle of the room, and there was a cheery, plump director supervising it all.

Pretty soon Mrs. Kennedy came down the stairs with her personal secretary. We were introduced, and then the director said, "O.K., Mrs. Kennedy? O.K., Dr. Spock? Just start talking and we'll start rolling." And both Mrs. Kennedy and I said, "Oh, but we haven't decided what we are going to talk about." He said, "You just start talking and we'll snip a little here and we'll snip a little there."

We couldn't be persuaded, so we sat there for an awkward few minutes before deciding that we were going to talk about the nursing shortage and some steps that might be taken to recruit more nurses. The camera rolled.

Mrs. Kennedy was a very good listener and a very good conversationalist. After the cameras stopped rolling, we both kept talking (though I remember doing the larger part). Finally the director had to shoo me out, "Time to go, Doctor." I never heard from anybody who'd seen the film.

Later I was asked to do another television stint as a citizen of Cleveland, Ohio welcoming Kennedy to the Youngstown airport. I was to climb up the ramp, enter the Senator's plane, and then back out for a handshaking ceremony for the TV cameras. But the plan misfired. As Kennedy emerged from the plane, the huge crowd roared its welcome, and he raised his arm to answer with a salute, not even noticing my outstretched hand. I resourcefully backed down one step and offered my hand again, just as the crowd roared again. We repeated the sequence like clockwork about ten times, and when we reached the ground, my handler said, "Never mind, we'll try again at the hotel," where Kennedy was to speak from the marquee over the entrance facing the city square.

The crowd at the hotel was really thick, and it took quite a while for the guide, Jane, my son John, and I to work our way into the lobby and up the one flight of stairs to Kennedy's suite. Police were swarming everywhere and stopping us every five paces. Finally we got into the small, plain suite. It was not a fancy hotel.

Kennedy was in the bedroom changing his shirt, but we were greeted by the governor of the state and by Pierre Salinger, Kennedy's press relations man. After a few minutes Kennedy emerged from the bedroom with his clean shirt on. He was obviously preoccupied with the speech he was about to give, and I had to remind him what I was there for. He said, "Get the press service photographers." Salinger snapped his fingers or rubbed a lamp, and instantly three press service photographers appeared. Kennedy sat down on a sofa, and I sat beside him. I could see that he was preoccupied and it would be up to me to make conversation. He asked, "Let's see, where are you working now?" and I said, "Western Reserve Medical School." Then, knowing that he was on the Board of Governors at Harvard, and grasping for something amusing to break the ice, I said, "You know, our new curriculum at Western Reserve is so popular that three people turned down *Harvard* Medical School this fall to come to Western Reserve." He replied solemnly, "You know, I'm on the Board of Governors there." So my sally had fallen flat.

Why did I support John Kennedy? I hadn't been radicalized by 1960. Kennedy's politics reflected my political thinking at that time. He was a mildly liberal Democrat, and I had not yet been disillusioned by the Democratic Party. I was still hawkish in my sympathies and I was scornful of the Eisenhower administration, particularly Dulles, the secretary of state, to whom Eisenhower delegated most decisions on foreign policy. And I believed that Eisenhower was economizing at the behest of George Humphrey, who was secretary of the Treasury and who dominated the overall domestic policy. I thought that Humphrey, who was a conservative, was just trying to save money on the defense budget. Kennedy said there was a missile gap, that Eisenhower's economizing was a dangerous way of trying to get "more bang for a buck." (After he was installed, Kennedy found that there was no missile gap.) I agreed.

For these two political chores for Kennedy, Jane and I were invited to the White House for a dinner of about a hundred and sixty people. This was a state dinner in honor of the Grand Duchess Charlotte of Luxembourg and her son, Prince William, who were on a state visit to the United States.

We arrived at the White House in an old borrowed Volkswagen; all around us were limousines. The doorman and a Capitol policeman indicated that I was to take the car down a certain drive for the equivalent of three city blocks and park it.

At the top of the red-carpeted marble stairs from that south portico to the main floor of the White House, a lieutenant colonel in the Marine Corps offered his arm to Jane and conducted us to the Blue Room, where people were assembling. As we got there he said, "When the reception line forms, you will fall in behind the Snows." The whole lineup was to be strictly alphabetical so that the announcer standing next to the president could just look at his list and know who was next. And then the lieutenant colonel said to me, "And at the point when you approach the president, the man steps in front of the woman." Jane was too preoccupied with looking around to hear him say this. (She referred to him afterward as "that flunky," and I said, "Jane, that's not a flunky, that's a lieutenant colonel in the Marine Corps.") We saw Rex Harrison and Helen Hayes there, and we saw Edward Steichen, the photographer who arranged the beautiful exhibit called *The Family of Man*. He had a new wife with him, very gorgeous and much younger than he. I remember thinking, By what right does that old geezer have such a beautiful young wife?

We heard a bugle note from way down the corridor, and in came the flag bearers, their guards, and President Kennedy and the Grand Duchess Charlotte, and behind came Prince William with Mrs. Kennedy. The receiving line began to move, and when we got within six feet of the president, I said to Jane, "Now this is where I step in front of you." And she said, "You will not!" I practically had to elbow her back into line behind me, because we were right next to the president. I swung around from this little quarrel, and the president said, "Good evening, Doctor." He introduced me to the grand duchess, who introduced me to her son, who introduced me to Jackie Kennedy. And Jackie Kennedy said—looking me right in the eye and speaking very meaningfully—"And so we meet again!" I thought, This is intensely personal, what does it mean? Then I realized that this must be her manner with all men. This is why she captivated General De Gaulle. But I liked it.

Pretty soon we all entered the dining room. Mrs. Kennedy had revolutionized state dining arrangements, which traditionally had always been at a huge, horseshoe-shaped table. But she realized that that's socially awkward, and substituted round tables of twelve. At the table that I was directed to was Mrs. John Steinbeck. The host for that table was the postmaster general. On my right was the wife of a columnist—worldly, charming, easy to talk with. On my left was a much younger, very beautiful woman who was pregnant, rather humorless, and wanted to talk about her forthcoming baby. Her gown was extraordinarily low cut.

After dinner we went back to the Blue Room, where by this time one hundred and sixty little gilt chairs were set up for a musicale. I think it showed a certain lack of humor on somebody's part that they had arranged a concert by a group called the Consort Players, who played Elizabethan music on Elizabethan instruments. Between selections the actor Basil Rathbone, with an extremely long face, would stand up, open his tooled-leather folder and read a sonnet in an overly dramatic voice. It gave me goose flesh. Many of the older men went to sleep on their slender gilt chairs.

I WAS LATER INVITED to the White House by Lyndon Johnson, before we fell out over Vietnam. Dinner at the White House was different with Johnson. In the first place, it was not a white but a black tie affair. The dinner was in honor of Harold Wilson, the British prime minister, shortly after Johnson was elected. I guess there were a hundred and fifty people there. Lynda Bird Johnson was greeting guests informally in the Blue Room where we were having cocktails. Instead of the solemn musicale that the Kennedys had put on, Johnson had the Marine Corps Band playing dance music. Mostly jazz.

Later, Lyndon Johnson first danced with his wife, and then he invited a stunning, very coquettish woman in a tight-fitting spangled, electric-blue dress who played up to him dramatically. He murmured little remarks to her, and she giggled and laughed, showing tremendous appreciation. A lot of bachelor Army, Navy, and Marine Corps officers were there making a stag line to keep things moving. I noticed that these men were trained to watch and see who was stuck and to come and unstick them. Of course, they never tried to unstick Johnson while he was with the dazzling creature in the electric-blue spangles.

*Three-piece suit with the gold watch chain.*

# 14

I GOT INTO the antiwar movement in several unplanned steps. If I'd had any idea where it was leading me, I might have paused, though I doubt that my conscience would have let me stop altogether.

In the late fifties the National Committee for a Sane Nuclear Policy (SANE), which was at that time working principally for a test ban treaty, invited me twice to join their National Committee. I told them, "I don't know anything about radiation. And besides, I reassure parents—I don't scare them." Homer Jack, the executive director, showed admirable persistence. He invited me a third time in 1962 and finally got into my conscience. I realized that if we didn't have a test ban treaty, more and more children, not only in America but around the world, would die of cancer and leukemia or be born with mental and physical defects from fallout radiation. So I saw that it was a pediatric issue.

In March 1962 I joined the SANE national board. Several weeks later William Bernbach, who was both on the board of SANE and a founding partner of the advertising firm Doyle, Dane and Bernbach, said that if I would write the copy, his firm would incorporate it in an advertisement for disarmament, and SANE would pay for a full page in the *New York Times*.

I had been thinking of various aspects of disarmament, especially since joining SANE, but I had never come near to formulating a rounded philosophy or program. I was excited—but also scared— at the prospect of having a whole page in the *New York Times* for my message. I wrote and erased, wrote and erased, feverishly and compulsively, every free moment for days. I ended up with a document of three thousand words. But then the advertising expert who worked with me said I shouldn't use more than two hundred words. And that I should remove anything that sounded argumentative—that it would interfere with acceptance. I was being asked to discard ninety percent of my creation. It felt like being asked to commit hara kiri. We finally picked out a simple but impassioned plea that we should stop quibbling about details and save our world from self-destruction. It went with a large picture of me looking down sadly at a trusting one-year-old. The caption said, "Dr. Spock is worried." I must say it was a moving message. It was eventually published in a hundred newspapers by local SANE groups. The most remarkable thing of all was that the child sat calmly on my examining table playing with my watch chain for an hour and a half while the photographer took hundreds and hundreds of shots.

President Kennedy was in favor of a test ban treaty, but he was unsure if he could persuade the Senate to ratify it even if he came to a reasonable agreement with the Soviet Union. So he asked Norman Cousins, a cochairman of SANE and the editor of the *Saturday Review of Literature*, among other disarmament leaders, to do his damnedest to get the American people to understand and to support the test ban treaty.

Within a year after I'd joined SANE, they voted me and Stuart Hughes cochairmen of the National Committee. I felt quite unready for such a position. I'd been a liberal and I'd been a New Dealer, but I hadn't followed the issues carefully enough to be familiar with radiation, disarmament, and international relations. The organization sought to influence public opinion, and they as-

**Dr. Spock is worried.**

*The SANE advertisement of 1962.*

sumed I could influence the parents. But you can't do that without making speeches, meeting the press, and writing papers. The whole thing made me nervous.

To be sure, I had given talks to PTAs, to nursery school parents, and at the Child Study Association in New York City, but to very sympathetic audiences and on topics on which I was the expert. On radiation and disarmament I certainly was no expert. I felt that the reporters all knew better than I and were just out to ask me questions that would expose my ignorance.

When I joined SANE, it was a big event for Cleveland SANE. They asked me to join the annual march from the University Circle region down to the public square the day before Easter Sunday. I was not used to demonstrating, and I felt self-conscious when radio and television reporters would come up and stick a microphone under my nose and ask me, "Doctor, what are you doing here?" as if I'd been caught doing something shameful. This was not a group of bold, well-dressed marchers. They were good people from all backgrounds who were using their Saturday afternoon for a good cause, but they were dressed in Saturday afternoon clothes that you would wear for cleaning out the garage or washing the car. There were a lot of children too, carrying home-made signs, and the result was a straggly kind of march. I didn't think we would be taken seriously looking like this. When we filed into the Public Square I was told that the detectives taking our individual pictures were the police subversive squad. It shocked me that marching for disarmament could be considered subversive.

A T FIRST I leaned heavily on the executives of SANE and consulted them every time I was to make a statement or speech. Gradually I acquired knowledge, experience, and self-assurance.

In 1967, four years after I became cochairman, I urged that the National Committee of SANE ought to participate in the upcoming

April's peace march in New York, which had been organized by other groups. The conservative majority of the Committee were opposed to joining a demonstration organized by other, more radical groups. Back in the fifties the House Un-American Activities Committee had sharply questioned some of its members and Norman Cousins had reacted by getting the committee to require a sort of loyalty oath for its members. Across the country people supported SANE through contributions and demonstrations. In many cities they formed local SANE groups. The loyalty oath was disruptive both to SANE's National Committee and to its locals.

The SANE National Committee had a relatively conservative majority. They had originally selected themselves, starting out with people like Clarence Pickett, a Quaker leader who was the first cochairman of SANE along with Norman Cousins. Norman Thomas was a leader of the Socialist Party and many times its presidential candidate. There were also Rabbi Isidore Hoffman, the Jewish chaplain of Columbia, William Butler, a lawyer and son of a Supreme Court Justice, Leonore Marshall, a poet, and Helen Gahagan Douglas, the former member of Congress from California whom Nixon unseated in his first political campaign: he called her a communist.

SANE had spread and grown when local groups interested in disarmament applied to the National Committee for charters. Where there were no groups, individuals applied directly to the National Committee. So the National Committee, really a national board, was then nominally presiding over locals all over the country that were, on the average, to the left of the SANE National Committee majority. Many college groups wanted to become SANE locals. The National Committee permitted this until they found out how frisky the undergraduates interested in disarmament were.

I thought the standoffishness toward other groups was dead wrong. I said that the peace movement was a popular movement, not a country club in which you felt entitled to blackball other people, and that the National Committee should officially sponsor

*Teaching at Western Reserve.*

the demonstration. This split the SANE National Committee, not quite down the middle. The majority were opposed to my position. I said at the committee meeting, "Well, I'm going to participate as an individual, and I'm not going to do it anonymously." All hell broke loose! Norman Cousins and the two executives of SANE rallied people who hadn't been to meetings in years. There was a motion to remove me that didn't quite pass. The conservatives certainly felt very hostile toward me. I marched and I spoke at the demonstration, which was huge and quite orderly. Even Norman Cousins later told me I had been right and he had been wrong; but he continued to oppose me and my position.

In the meantime, I had been participating in the deliberations of the National Conference for New Politics, a conglomerate of more or less radical people who were joining together to raise money for independent regional political movements, particularly black groups. The goal was an independent, left, national movement.

On Labor Day weekend in 1967 the groups put on a big, stormy conference at the Palmer House in Chicago—two thousand delegates and another two thousand observers. The black caucus, putting into action the new concept of "black power," absented themselves from the conference and effectively stalled it for two days while they formulated their "nonnegotiable demands": equal black votes and cochairmanship in all committees and plenary sessions. This deviation from democratic tradition outraged many participants, who took turns denouncing them at the microphone. But a considerable majority, concerned with forming a partnership with black groups at all costs, voted to accept. The black caucus then demanded acceptance of thirteen platform planks; most controversial of all was a "condemnation of Israeli aggression," which caused even more impassioned debate, though it was eventually accepted.

Another prolonged and grim debate was that between advocates of community organizing and of electoral politics—as if the use of one ruled out the other. The wrangles seemed to me to be a tragic example of the tendency of some liberals and radicals to hurl themselves into furious, divisive arguments that sometimes destroy whole movements. I had made a speech the first day of the conference begging the delegates to avoid this kind of political suicide, but it was too much to ask.

Jim Rollins, a young black delegate, and I were elected cochairmen of the organization. I was now ready for this degree of radicalism; I was impatient with the timid majority of the SANE National Committee and attracted to the broader, bolder aims of New Politics. As it turned out, the plank condemning Israeli aggression dried up most of the funding sources and the organization soon withered away. But my participation was too much even for my supporters on the National Committee of SANE. We agreed amicably that it would be better for me to choose, so I resigned my cochairmanship and my membership on the National Committee of SANE in September 1967.

Thereafter I had no official position with SANE. I paid my dues but I attended no meetings. I never *publicly* called attention to my resignation from the cochairmanship and the National Committee of SANE, and the press happened not to notice it.

SANE contacted me again in 1980. They had become quite a different organization under a different executive. The old suspicions about me had gradually evaporated, and the Washington headquarters of SANE offered space and facilities to other national organizations that were sympathetic to SANE. They named the building The Ben Spock Peace Center, and I was glad to make a little speech when they dedicated it.

IN THE SUMMER of 1964 Lyndon Johnson's campaign committee invited me to support him on radio and television in his bid for election. I told them I certainly would, both as a citizen and as a spokesman for the disarmament movement, because he had said while campaigning in the spring and summer of 1964, "I will not send American boys to fight in an Asian war." (Kennedy had sent twenty thousand "military advisers.") I went on radio and television in his support. One half-hour television commercial I participated in featured President Kennedy's science adviser, Jerome Wiesner, who became dean of science at M.I.T., an admiral who had been head of the CIA, Professor George Kistiakowsky of Harvard, and about five other people. We sat around a table denouncing Goldwater for his rash belligerence and pointing with pride to Lyndon Johnson, whom we called a statesman for promising not to get us further involved in the war in Vietnam. We were told that Lyndon Johnson loved this television commercial so much, with all these distinguished people calling him a statesman, that he had it shown several times at the White House.

Within a couple of days after his successful election Johnson himself called me up at Western Reserve Medical School to thank me for my help in electing him president. He added, "I hope I will prove worthy of your trust," and I said, "Oh, President Johnson, of course you will!" It never occurred to me that he would betray our trust so badly and so swiftly.

It was only three months later, in February 1965, that he abruptly turned our Vietnam involvement into full-scale war: he began the bombing of North Vietnam and the buildup of fighting troops that eventually reached a half-million, of whom 57,000 died. I was afraid that it would lead to World War III at any time. The Soviet Union and China both threatened to come into the war— the Soviet Union if we mined Haiphong Harbor, and China if we bombed Hanoi.

I wrote Johnson several indignant letters. I got replies from McGeorge Bundy, Johnson's national-security adviser. Bundy was a very condescending correspondent, and his letters took the following tone: "My dear Doctor, you may be assured that we have considered the point of view that you express, and we feel that it has no validity whatsoever."

Next I sent a letter via one of the president's assistants, asking him to put it on Johnson's desk. In this letter I told Johnson that he was utterly wrong from every point of view. That Vietnam was one country, not two: That he was wrong to think he could win when the French had so ignominiously failed. That our reactionary puppet Diem was hated. That the war violated the Constitution, which says that only Congress can declare war. That the American people would turn against the war and bring the Republican Party back into power. There were ten points in all. This time Johnson himself replied, but he took up just one point: where I had accused him, too broadly, of going totally against his promise not to send Americans to fight in an Asian war. (He brought up the Tonkin Gulf Resolution in which he had threatened retaliation.) He ended his letter by saying, "I hope that I may have your support in the future." That unleashed another long letter from me, in which I told him rather rudely, why he couldn't expect my support.

At this time, I was still enough·in the good graces of the administration to be invited to take part in the White House Conference on International Cooperation. I watched Johnson carefully when he shook hands with me, he didn't change his facial expression one bit. At the climax of his speech at that conference, Secretary of State Dean Rusk, revealed what I thought was the fatuousness of our policy toward Vietnam, China and the U.S.S.R. by leaning forward toward the two thousand guests from all over the world, and twice intoning, "Communist nations have *appetite*! Communist nations have *appetite*!" It sounded like a scout master telling a ghost story at the campfire. It was the U.S. that had gone half way around the world to try to control Southeast Asia.

I wrote to Jerome Wiesner after Johnson's escalation, suggesting that we get as many of those panelists as possible, most of whom we knew were opposed to what Johnson was doing, to write a group letter to him. I thought it would impress Johnson that the people who had supported him now thought that he was going haywire in Vietnam. Wiesner felt it was all right for us to protest as individuals but not to make this statement as a group. I still think it was worth doing. But I didn't have enough self-assurance to go ahead and collect the other people's signatures.

*Rally for Welfare Rights, Boston Common, 1969.*

# 15

I DON'T THINK that I had any special power when it came to changing minds. Young people simply didn't want to be sent to Vietnam to kill and be killed in a war that they considered all wrong. It was young people who carried the main burden of opposition to the war, overwhelmingly so at demonstrations. But they still wanted the backing of older people at rallies and in talks, and that's where I came in. I was a responsible professional person and was vehemently opposed to the war on a military, moral, and constitutional basis.

This made me a popular speaker. My schedule for a number of years was every other month on the road. I spoke six days a week, sometimes seven, at a different university every day. Often there was a press conference at the airport and interviews on television, in the afternoon. Toward the end of the afternoon I was usually asked to make myself available in the student lounge for informal discussions. Then I'd have dinner with the students. Usually I'd give the talk from eight to nine and answer questions from nine to ten, and then they would announce to those who had additional questions that I would be available in the student lounge. About eleven my handlers would say, "Now we're going to Professor Jenkins's house, where we can really relax." *They* could relax, because their job of arranging everything had been accomplished, but for me it was the hardest session of all. Here students would ask me fundamental questions like "Do you think I should go to Canada, or do you think I should go to jail?"—questions that my psychological training told me I shouldn't even try to answer. If a person can't make up his own mind about such crucial matters of conscience, somebody else whom he trusts would only get him more mixed up by telling him what to do. Such students I would simply draw out more in a conversation, crumpled up on the couch at Professor Jenkins's house and sweating like a horse at this stage. Finally at midnight I would say to my student handlers, "I've got to get to the motel and sleep because I'm getting up at six to catch the first plane out."

One of the things that preoccupied me on the road was how to keep my clothes looking neat. I always carried an extra suit and managed to jam in four or five shirts, eight or ten detachable collars, shorts, and maybe an extra pair of shoes all in a carry-on bag. Back at the motel I would try to take the worst wrinkles out of my suit by pressing a hot wet washcloth against the elbow and knee wrinkles and, if possible, hang the suit up high to dry on the chandelier or curtain rod.

In my speeches I ended up trying to give people a sense of their own power. I would try to persuade those who were only half-persuaded that it's right to protest a war like that. I began by telling them how I was born and raised a Republican, that my father was a Republican who revered Coolidge and that in my first election, in 1924, I just assumed his political views were right, and voted a straight Republican ticket. My audiences were composed mostly of liberal students and faculty, so the idea that I had started as an unthinking Republican amused them and kept them from dismissing me as a cranky radical from birth. It showed them that it's possible to change.

Then I'd explain the history of our involvement in Vietnam—the thing they had come to hear. I went back to France's colonialization of Indochina in the nineteenth century, the Japanese occupation in World War II, and the resistance that Ho Chi Minh led against the Japanese and later the French. The Vietnamese defeated the French at Dien Bien Phu. The peace treaty, called the Geneva Accords, specified that Vietnam would be divided into North and South for just two years, to allow the French to settle their affairs. Then the country was to be reunited and national elections held—no more foreign intervention. The U.S. promised at Geneva to abide by these terms. Even President Eisenhower admitted that Ho Chi Minh would win the election by eighty percent. But then, breaking our government's promise, the Catholic archbishop of New York, Joe Kennedy, father of John, and Secretary of State Dulles got together and had the U.S. install its first puppet government in the South, under Diem. Later John Kennedy kept it in power by sending twenty thousand so-called military advisers.

I explained how I supported Lyndon Johnson on television and radio in 1964 because he promised not to send Americans to fight in an Asian war, and how he betrayed us. I told them how the FBI had lied about me, how they didn't understand American democracy and really thought it was their business to be suspicious of anybody who didn't agree politically with J. Edgar Hoover. An FBI man was always visible in the middle of the audience, in his slouch hat and his camel hair coat. At one peace rally when everybody was asked to get up and hold hands in a circle and sing, the two FBI agents were left sitting in the middle, sticking out like sore thumbs.

Then I would go on to the question "Does anything do any good?" and gave them my strenuous belief that any actions *do* do good. I'd point out that opposition to the war was growing. When Lyndon

*Protest march in New York City.*

Johnson declined to run again, I made the most of it: the most powerful man in the twentieth century had proved incapable of stemming the tide.

I always got a standing ovation when I finished, and that gave me encouragement to keep going.

*Front page of the* New York Post, *December 5, 1967.*

# 16

SOME PEOPLE HAVE the impression that I commit civil disobedience often. I calculate that in a twenty-five-year period I have
engaged in it a dozen times, so that averages only about once every
two years. I don't protest *just* with civil disobedience. I vote carefully. I write letters frequently, not only to the president but to
my representative and my senators, and to newspaper editors. I
lobby in Washington and at the local offices of officeholders. I
attend demonstrations. And from time to time I commit civil
disobedience.

I never went around looking for opportunities to commit civil
disobedience. I was brought up to be excessively respectful of the
authorities. It took me a long while to agree to commit non-violent
civil disobedience—what held me back wasn't guilt but anxiety. It
still makes me uncomfortable inside. But organizations know that
a well-known, white-haired pediatrician in a three-piece suit getting arrested will help get the right attention, so they recruit me.
And if it's a good cause, my fear of nuclear weapons or my outrage
about homeless people or my anger at racial injustice is greater
than my fear of being arrested.

The whole point of any demonstration, obedient or disobedient, is to impress other people and the government with the strength of your conviction. That's probably the main reason I participate in civil disobedience—to show how strongly I disapprove of government actions that I think are criminal and to try to persuade them to the same view and to the same action. Civil disobedience has an honorable history. The Boston Tea Party, which played an important role in involving our people in the Revolution and which is included approvingly in our children's history books, was civil disobedience. Gandhi led the movement that drove the British out of India with non-violent civil disobedience. The example of Daniel and Phillip Berrigan was most effective in involving me in civil disobedience. I thought that if priests could bring themselves to break into government offices, steal draft records, and spatter them with duck blood, then I shouldn't be scared of committing milder forms of disobedience.

I had no idea, when I joined SANE in 1962 that I would become a full-time opponent of a war, but I never thought it was a mistake. Generally, people had one of three reactions to my participation in politics. First, some people lost all confidence in me and were rather indignant. A few of them wrote to me, "I'll never believe a word you say." Those, I think were a relative minority. A much larger group of people disagreed with me (at least initially) about Vietnam and disapproved of my political activity, especially civil-disobedience demonstrations, yet still believed that *Baby and Child Care* was a wise book—that it was just too bad I had stepped into the wrong role. And then there were people who thought that not only was it a good book but I was a good man to risk my reputation taking what was at first an unpopular stand.

M Y FIRST ARREST was in October 1967 in New York City with Dave McReynolds, who was head of the War Resisters' League. Dave, knowing that the young people were going to have several days of civil disobedience at the Whitehall Street Induction

Center, thought that it would be a good idea for older people to demonstrate too. So he and I had a conference with Mayor Lindsay and Chief Inspector of Police Garelik. We told them of our plans to block the steps of the induction center on Whitehall Street. It was only to be a symbolic blocking. We would not really interfere with the arriving drafters.

We promised no violence and asked that the police not chase and club our people the way they had done a couple of weeks before to those who were demonstrating outside a hotel against Secretary of State Dean Rusk, who was to make a speech there.

I appeared at Whitehall Street at five o'clock in the morning, where there were two thousand demonstrators, mostly middle-aged citizens. And five thousand policemen were surrounding the induction center behind barriers, the kind used to close a street to traffic. I was to lead the demonstrators who were willing to be arrested. Dave said that Chief Inspector Garelik would give him a signal when the time was right. Then we could climb *under* the barriers and approach the steps of the Whitehall Street Induction Center. I guess that going under the barriers was to slow us down.

Dave said that I should lead the demonstrators to the front of the induction center, right up to the police barrier. Other demonstrators who couldn't afford the time to be arrested were going to stay across the street, on the sidewalk. At least half of the two thousand demonstrators followed me right up to the barrier. There were a lot of press, radio, and television people. It was still pitch dark and those five thousand policemen facing us with the street-light glinting on their badges made an awesome sight. The media people began asking me, "Doctor, what are you going to do?" And I wasn't sure how it would turn out, so I thought it better not to make any promises.

All the demonstrators behind me kept pushing up front to see what the action was so I was being pressed against the barriers. We stayed there ten, twenty, thirty minutes, with the press constantly asking me what our plans were, but no word came from McReynolds. Of course, if I'd had the experience I have now, I would have gladly used that time to explain not only what the tentative plan was but why we were objecting to the Vietnam War.

Finally I decided we couldn't keep that up forever. Something had gone wrong with the communications, a leader is meant to lead. So I abruptly dropped to my knees and tried to get under the barrier. The police were thick behind the barrier. They closed ranks, so that I was up against a solid phalanx of police shins. I tried butting a little to the left and a little to the right to find an opening, but I couldn't find one. I realized, I can't carry out my mission. What am I going to say to the press? To use up time, I brushed the dust off and straightened out my Homburg hat.

Then I stood up, to a barrage of questions, but I had no answers. I moved a few yards to my right and then abruptly dropped to my knees, thinking I could get through before the police could close ranks in front of me. But it was no use. Then I thought maybe it would be better to climb over the barrier, which was simply saw-horses with planks running between them. As I got to the top and tried to lean forward to jump down on the other side, the police simply reached up and pushed me backward, while I grasped the cuffs of their coats. I was moving further to the right to see if I could find another opening when, in a strange way, as in a dream, the police ranks thinned out in front of me and revealed an open space with Chief Inspector Garelik in the middle.

I was so frustrated and humiliated by my failure as a leader that I took on the manner of a five-year-old who has been promised a lollipop and hasn't received it. "Inspector Garelik," I whined, "I want to commit civil disobedience!" He moved a little closer to me and in a low, conspiratorial tone said, "If you move farther down to the right to the corner of this block, you will find a way to get through." I followed these instructions, squeezing my way along the barriers. Sure enough, there at the streetcorner was a gap just wide enough for one person to get through. I slipped through and was challenged by a police officer, who said in a loud ceremonial tone, "Do you have business at the induction center?" This was a part of the scenario that I hadn't heard about; I didn't

*In a paddy wagon in Washington, D.C.*

know the right answer. But I didn't want to be frustrated again. In a loud voice I said, *"I certainly do."* He didn't offer any other objection, and I walked twenty paces to the steps of the induction center and sat down. I was promptly arrested and led to a police van just a few steps away. Gradually my followers, who were coming through the same gap, also got arrested, and eventually the van filled up and went trundling and bumping away. This was the first time I had the strange feeling of being closed in a van with no idea in which direction we were going.

The Tombs is the detention center in downtown New York. We were led through corridors into an area with heavy bars up to the ceiling. It occupied part of a large room, and our busload was put in this pen. Then we saw other busloads being led to other pens.

It was all men in this room. They detained the women in another place. Something I learned about being arrested for civil disobedience is that there are long, long waits. Waits to be searched, waits to give identification data, waits to be fingerprinted, waits to be mugged (photographed), and then just plain waiting with nothing to read. One of my penmates was the poet Allen Ginsberg, who taught us all to meditate. We were all chanting, "OMMMMM . . ." A strange place to meditate.

Finally, after what seemed like hours and hours and hours, we were led before a judge and asked how we pled. I thought about pleading not guilty, because the trial was going to be in New York City, where I was living. It's always worthwhile pleading not guilty if it's convenient to go back for trial. You may win on a technicality. If not, you have to plead nolo contendere, which means "I don't want a trial but I don't admit I'm guilty either." You put up twenty-five-dollars' bail that turns into a fine if you don't appear. My participation at Whitehall was to have repercussions in my life, as I found out shortly.

WHENEVER I TALK to audiences about civil disobedience, I advise enlisting at least a few clergymen, for two reasons: it's morally reassuring to have clergymen being arrested with you, and it disconcerts the police. I've seen policemen trembling with anxiety to have to nab and jail clergymen.

I remember one D.C. demonstration where a hundred and fifty clergymen were arrested for committing civil disobedience which consisted of staying in the rotunda of the Capitol after 4:30 P.M. As each bus filled up with clergymen and started off, they were in high spirits—naughty boys at last, after being goody-goody all their adult lives. They were shouting and singing, and when they saw a pedestrian coming down the street, they would stick their arms out between the bars and give the "V" sign. The look on the pedestrians' faces was incredulous—busloads of clergymen going off to jail!

At the jail they take away everything that you have in your pockets, and also your necktie, for fear you will hang yourself. Coffee is usually available, though it often runs out before everybody gets served. Most often the solid food, if any, is a frozen baloney sandwich that obviously has been sitting around for a long time waiting for a customer. I still remember the crunch it makes when you bite into it.

The singing of the hundred and fifty clergymen arrested in the rotunda was particularly wonderful because there were so many of them, and clergymen in general are very good singers from years of leading the singing in their churches. They know not only the first verse but often the second and third verses as well. And they sing boldly, so that the hymns echo up and down the cellblock. The acoustics in the jail are perfect for singing because everything is concrete; there's no carpet, and there are no curtains because there are no windows.

You usually sleep without a mattress on a metal bunk. But if the group is large, some will have to sleep on the concrete floor. The police don't want to be too hospitable to people who deliberately make trouble for them. It is usually not until the next day that they take you into court.

WHILE I'VE NEVER been abused myself during an arrest, I have seen it happen to others. I was arrested along with thousands during the big May Day 1971 demonstrations in Washington. There were two huge demonstrations. The legal one, which involved three-quarters of a million people, was followed a day or two later by a large civil-disobedience action with about fifty thousand. The theme of the civil disobedience was "Let's close the Pentagon." The idea was that by blocking traffic in Washington we could make it impossible for some people working at the Pentagon to get to work and back.

I was assigned to a group that assembled at six o'clock in the morning near the Washington Monument, and we were to cross the 16th Street Bridge to the Pentagon. We tried to march directly toward the bridge, but large numbers of police blocked our way. So we decided to use one of the indirect approaches to the bridge. We had no trouble at first. We thought we had outwitted the police. We went up a ramp onto the approach to the bridge. Suddenly the police came charging after us, throwing mace. The policeman who threw the mace bomb toward our particular group looked wildly excited. They soon had us surrounded and arrested.

I was in jail by 7:00 A.M. I was chagrined later to find that Herb Magidson, my peace activist friend from Beverly Hills, and Noam Chomsky, the linguistics professor from M.I.T., and their group had succeeded in evading arrest all day long. They would lie down in an intersection and block traffic until they saw the police coming or heard sirens. Then they would leap up and run off to do the same thing at another intersection.

When we were arrested, we were first taken to a holding pen in a courthouse basement, then a little later put back in paddy wagons and taken to the Redskins' practice field, which was surrounded by a high wire fence. The police had prudently taken it over for the occasion. There were something like four or five thousand people in this field.

Supporters on the outside brought packages of cookies and bread and salami and threw them over the top of the fence. But there was not nearly enough for all. Makeshift toilets (fence tarpaulins and fifty-gallon drums) were politely segregated for men and women. A tent was rigged so that some of us could keep out of the drizzle and the cold. A couple got married in the playing field that day. There were plenty of clergyman about and no doubt plenty of couples in love, but it was an unusual place for a wedding.

Somebody brought me over to see Abbie Hoffman in a first-aid tent that the prisoners had improvised. He was lying on the ground, his face badly cut and bruised. He said that a motorcycle policeman had spotted him, run him down, then come back and run over his face a couple of times more. He looked it.

I was called over to one side of this large enclosure where the press were assembled outside the fence and was interviewed through the wire mesh. When I visited Hanoi several years later, after U.S. troops had been withdrawn from Vietnam, I saw in a museum a blown-up photograph of me in the Redskins' field, giving the clenched-fist salute for a photographer.

Attorney General John Mitchell arranged for these mass arrests without any legal procedures whatsoever. Our names were not taken, nor fingerprints nor photographs. A number of people decided to sue the government and the attorney general for illegal arrest. I must admit that it was satisfying when Mitchell himself was eventually charged, tried, found guilty, and sent to jail for his part in Watergate. I thought he had it coming.

Late in the afternoon they began removing thousands of us pris oners from the Redskins' field and putting us in an indoor hockey rink. It was getting really cold by dark. Sometime during the night they began processing us. You could go and plead and put up your twenty-five-dollar bail and go home. I needed to get back to New York, so I paid my bail. Finally, at 3:00 A.M., I found a taxi and went to the Washington airport and stayed in one of those overnight sleeping cells, like a berth on a pullman car, and took the first plane out to New York at 6:00 A.M.

TWICE I'VE BEEN ASKED to join civil-disobedience actions by Mitch Snyder with the Community for Creative Non-Violence in Washington, D.C. In the first year of the Reagan administration Mary and I were arrested for kneeling in front of the White House in protest against cuts in medical funding for children and old people. More recently Mary and I joined them in a demonstration for the homeless. Mitch Snyder is an effective and dedicated person. He and the others in the CCNV live with the poor they are serving. Their main activity is to go out and collect leftover food at markets and restaurants and then prepare a stew for thousands of homeless people in Washington.

I would be ashamed to turn down their request. I am only a

dilettante in civil-disobedience demonstrations. Other people organize them and I come and briefly participate. But it takes more dedication than I have to live month after month, year after year in a decrepit building, serving homeless people. I don't even join fasts using my age as an excuse.

I wear a suit when I'm arrested. I think it helps to remind people that this isn't a rowdy act but a carefully considered demonstration that I deem worthy of great respect. When we were arrested at the Seneca Army Depot at Romulus, New York, in October 1983, I had on a good suit and didn't want to tear it on the barbed wire, so I was grateful that someone had brought along a towel: I draped it on the barbed wire and climbed over.

This was the only time I was arrested by troops of the United States Army. The arresting officers were very helpful, very polite. As we dropped down from the top of the barbed-wire fence, they

*Arrested for protesting cuts in housing budget, Washington, D.C.,*
*November 7, 1988.*

gave us a hand to make sure we didn't hurt ourselves. They addressed me as "sir."

I compare that to an incident in Washington, D.C., on June 2, 1982. They strip-searched my wife Mary, squat-searched her, and sprayed her for lice and crabs, though they did not do this to the men. It was sexist discrimination. I was proud that she sued the Washington police and city government and even prouder that after she won her suit, the police were not allowed to squat-search or strip-search women prisoners unless there was a justifiable suspicion that they might be harboring drugs—certainly not for being in a political demonstration. Mary sued for half a million dollars and was awarded four hundred, which, incidentally, she hasn't seen yet.

*David Levine's cartoon comment on the indictment.*

# 17

BACK IN DECEMBER of 1967 the FBI called me up and said they would like to come and talk to me about my antiwar activities. I was ingenuous. I said, "I've been writing to the president and my senators and my congressmen again and again, and they don't seem to understand my position. Come on over and I'll tell you exactly how I feel." I found out later that I didn't have to let them come. Still, I don't like the idea of saying "no comment" or "I have nothing to say." It sounds as if I'm trying to conceal something.

Two FBI men appeared at the door. One of them was somewhat more mature—he was the interrogator. The other man was the scribe. I was very hospitable and cordial. I cleared my desk for the scribe because, as I told him, I hate to write in my lap. I should have known they were there to hang something on me. I should have said something sassy like "The FBI doesn't understand our form of government or the Constitution, which says that the people are entitled to speak on and hear all sides of issues. The FBI teaches that anyone who disagrees with J. Edgar Hoover's politics is subversive." But, instead, during this interview I talked a blue streak about how I had become involved in the antiwar movement and why I opposed the war. At one point the scribe's fingers became cramped from writing, and he laid down his pen and wrung his hands. I said impatiently, "Get this down! I want you to get it down!"

In January 1968, a month or more after this friendly visit, five of us were indicted by the Department of Justice for conspiracy to counsel, aid, and abet resistance to the draft: Reverend William Sloane Coffin, Jr., the chaplain at Yale; Marcus Raskin, codirector of the Institute for Policy Studies; Mitchell Goodman, a writer; Michael Ferber, a graduate student; and myself.

B ACK IN THE LATE SPRING and early summer of 1967, a number of activists from all over the country had composed a document titled "A Call to Resist Illegitimate Authority." It had been passed around and lots of people made suggestions, but Marcus Raskin did the main writing and editing of it. In it we said that the war in Vietnam was illegal and unconstitutional because there had never been a declaration of war by Congress. The closest thing to that was the Tonkin Gulf Resolution. In it the Johnson administration, claiming that the North Vietnamese had made an unprovoked attack on our naval forces in the Gulf of Tonkin, asked for—and got—Congressional authorization to repel such aggression in the future. (The Pentagon Papers later showed very clearly that the president, the secretaries of defense and state, and the national security advisor had all discussed some way of provoking the North Vietnamese into some kind of action to achieve exactly this result. The papers showed too that such an attack may never have taken place; the Navy had reported that North Vietnamese gunboats had approached and launched torpedos, but this report was dubious, and in any case no torpedos had ever hit any of our naval vessels.)

In speaking of our government's many war crimes in Vietnam, our document invoked the Nuremberg Principle, under which the Allies had tried and put to death Germans and Japanese for crimes against the peace, crimes against humanity, and war crimes in the aftermath of World War II. When the Germans and Japanese objected that they had simply been following the orders of their superiors, our judges at the Nuremberg trials said that was no excuse: if they knew or believed that they were being ordered to commit crimes against the peace, crimes against humanity, or war crimes, they were not only entitled but *obligated* to refuse to obey such orders. Americans, we said, are likewise obligated to refuse to be inducted to fight a war full of such crimes. Our idea was to get tens of thousands of signatures from people coast to coast, especially in universities and colleges, in support of our declaration.

I was one of the early signers and sponsors of "A Call to Resist Illegitimate Authority." I answered my wife's fears of incrimination by saying, "Oh, they wouldn't be so foolish as to go after an old pediatrician like me."

I WAS ALWAYS SLOW at figuring things out. I was at the office of Pocket Books when the news came out that I had been indicted. But I didn't know about it until the end of my meeting, when I went to a public telephone and called home. Jane said excitedly, "Do you know you're indicted? Come home immediately and don't speak to anybody. The lobby of the apartment house is full of reporters." I was taken aback, and I started for the subway.

What was I indicted for and why couldn't I comment? I tried to call Jane again to ask, at Penn Station and at Times Square, but the line was busy. A man on the subway had a *New York Post* with the huge headline "Spock Indicted," but the rest was too small to read. I thought of asking him to lend it to me for a minute, but I realized he'd think I was a nut.

I took the shuttle across to Grand Central and went into a phone booth to call home, and the line was busy. I took the Lexington Avenue subway up to 86th Street and tried to call home from there. The line was busy. I saw that I'd have to decide on my own. I imagined the lobby of the apartment house full of press. As I walk in and they leap forward, sticking microphones in my face, I will say to them, "Gentlemen, let me have five minutes with my wife and I'll come back down and talk to you." As I rounded the corner of 83rd Street, I held my head proudly erect and walked into the lobby, but there wasn't a soul there except the doorman. All the newsmen had been discouraged so emphatically by Jane that they had all gone home.

I knew I needed a good lawyer. Cora Weiss, one of the more prominent activists I'd worked with, and who had organized several large demonstrations in New York City and Washington, D.C., said of course I should have Leonard Boudin represent me. I'd gotten to know Leonard's daughter, Kathy—a true radical—three years earlier in Cleveland. I called him and he said, "I thought, what with the news in tonight's papers, someone would be calling me." I liked Leonard's casual style and his humor. He advised me to admit to the press only what was already public knowledge. He agreed to represent me.

Jane had a long list of papers and radio and television stations I was to call. I told them to come around to the apartment at 8:00 P.M. It was quite a sight. The apartment was of fair size, and it was absolutely jammed with television, radio, and newspaper people. Never had I been the center of such clamorous attention. I realized how difficult it is at, say, a presidential press conference to decide whose question comes next. As soon as I finished a sentence, twenty people raised their hands and shouted questions at me. They don't discipline themselves; it's up to the interviewee to do the controlling. I gradually learned to point to the journalist who was being most aggressive. As soon as I would answer his question, there would be another twenty. And in the frenzy I did admit something that made at least a slight difference at the trial.

The next day the five indictees got together. I thought they would all use Leonard, but it eventually became apparent that they weren't going to join together. Every one of the five wanted to have separate counsel, and by the time the trial began, each had accumulated two to five lawyers of his own. Our strategy meetings were really crowded. Of course, it would have been less expensive for all of us and more efficient at the trial to have just one person running the show, but that's the egotism of opinionated liberals.

The government's position was that we were not only speaking against the war but also encouraging the resistance of draftees. The specific charges were conspiracy to counsel draft resisters, aiding them (offering moral support), and abetting them (raising money for their legal defense). The government's indictment pointed to five actions. First, we had circulated "A Call to Resist Illegitimate Authority," in which we offered to raise money for the defense of draft resisters. Second, we had held a press conference with a dozen other antiwar people and made vigorous attacks on our government for its war crimes, crimes against the peace, and crimes against humanity. Third, we had participated in a draft card burning ceremony at the Arlington Street Church in Boston. Fourth, we had delivered the burnt cards to the attorney general in Washington, D.C. And fifth, we had participated in civil disobedience by symbolically blocking the entrance to the Whitehall Street Induction Center in New York City. The government wanted to show that it was not just words we were dealing with—that our words had led to action. In our law that's an important distinction. It may not be a crime to discuss or advocate something, but if it leads to a criminal action, that is indictable.

I had no idea when I joined SANE in 1962 that this would lead me to becoming a spokesman for an antiwar movement, to civil disobedience, and to indictment for a federal crime. First I had supported an antiwar candidate for the presidency. Then we were betrayed by him. Next he had me and four others indicted for what I would call just telling the truth to the American people. I never thought of myself as a traitor; I felt that my position was more moral than the government's. But it did make me unhappy to have many people turn against me.

Our first defense strategy was to claim that the war was unconstitutional, illegal, and full of war crimes, and to invoke the Nuremberg Principle. This should have been a political trial, of course, not a criminal one. But the judge, Francis Ford—an old coot of eighty-three—said on the very first day of trial that since the legality or illegality of the war was not justifiable, there was to be no talk about that. We were greatly hamstrung by this ruling as to what kinds of testimony and evidence we could bring into court. So we had to use another line of defense.

None of the other four had a lawyer identified with anti-government and radical issues like Leonard Boudin. Their lawyers assumed they'd been retained to get their clients off. (Ironically, Marcus Raskin's chief lawyer was Telford Taylor, the prosecutor in the Nuremberg trials.) As a result, the defendants were made to seem on the defensive about their participation in the antiwar movement. We heard that some of the leaders of the movement deplored this legal quibbling. They thought we should be using the trial as a forum to voice our beliefs, explain our political activities, and attack the government on the war. So as the last of the five to take the stand, I didn't wait for the prosecutor to try to get me in a corner; I quickly admitted my participation in all the activities charged and went on to say that I believed the war was totally wrong and that was why I was doing everything possible to get people to force the government to end it. This line required close cooperation with Leonard, who understood well the purposes of a political trial.

By and large, however, it was a very frustrating and dull trial. Most of the evidence was newsreel film that showed us addressing crowds, participating in ceremonies where draft cards were burned, and committing civil disobedience at the induction center in New York. We already knew we had done these things, so there was no surprise in seeing them on film. Parts of it were so boring that I sometimes went to sleep after lunch, and I think some other defendants did too. I must say, I was surprised that somebody brought up as goody-goody as I was could go to sleep at my own trial for a federal crime. But the shades were always pulled down in the courtroom to show these films, which was done right after lunch: it was a soporific situation. Besides, I think that being on trial with four other people, all of them idealists and one of them a clergyman, kept me from feeling that I as an individual had committed a crime.

The only enjoyable aspect of our trial had to do with the testimony of the FBI interrogator who had come to my apartment. He had been feeling sick and was somewhat groggy when he came to the trial. First he testified from memory. Two-thirds of what he said was true; the rest was made up. Referring to his official FBI report on the interview, he said that I had told them that my main purpose was "to interfere with the levying of troops." But I would never have used the archaic phrase "levying of troops." Besides, I had said that my main purpose in all the demonstrations was to call the attention of the American people to the illegality, unconstitutionality, and criminality of the war in Vietnam and spur them to demand an end to it.

When he ended his testimony, he left his raw notes on the witness table—the ones the scribe made in my apartment, as opposed to the official report which he used in his testimony. Leonard and I noticed them right away. At his earliest opportunity, Leonard asked the U.S. Attorney if we could examine them in a private room, and we did so. Leonard then used the agent's notes as a basis for his cross-examination. There was nothing in them that said my main purpose was to interfere with the levying of troops.

The next day in court, this FBI agent was up for cross-examination by Leonard Boudin. When it came to discussing this material on the levying of troops, Leonard said, "I would like to have you read from the crude notes about the 'levying of troops.'" The FBI agent, of course, couldn't find it in the crude notes. He hemmed and hawed and fussed and shuffled the papers. But it wasn't there.

Leonard was always extremely suave and gentle, even when his questioning was technically quite aggressive. This was the first time I had ever seen him become openly aggressive, like the prosecutor in a movie trial. "There's nothing there, is there? You can't find it, can you? It's not there!" The FBI agent got more and more flustered. I think we made the point, at least with the jury, that they had falsified the testimony.

At one point when we were watching newsreel footage of demonstrations the prosecutor said to the projectionist, "Stop the film!" and then: "Gentlemen of the jury, did you see that face that appeared between Spock's and Coffin's shoulders? That was defendant Raskin." Marcus Raskin was distinctly shorter than Bill and I, so in some of these films he was not visible. While we would seize every opportunity to make statements about the evils of the war in Vietnam, he didn't shoot his mouth off the way we did. He was quieter in public. And every time any scene from these movies was shown, his lawyer would stand up and say, "And my client, Raskin, was not there, was he?" He made this statement so many times that it certainly impressed the jury.

The judge asked the jury to decide separate verdicts for each of us and to fill out a questionnaire breaking down for each defendant the single conspiracy charge into the three categories of conspiracy to counsel, conspiracy to aid, and conspiracy to abet. When the jury foreman was asked to read the verdicts, each defendant was asked to stand. For four of us the foreman said "guilty" on two of the three counts; no evidence had been presented as to counseling. We each stood proudly and with a slight smile—none of us felt guilty, and we didn't act guilty. But when it came to Marcus Raskin, he was pronounced "not guilty" on all three counts. Instead of smiling he turned ashen pale, rushed from the courtroom, and took the elevator to the ground floor of the federal courthouse, which was also the Boston Post Office. The press were not allowed in the courtroom, so they were all downstairs in this building waiting to hear the verdict. The first thing they knew, the elevator door opened and out sprang Marcus, shaken and with tears on his face. It was perplexing to the press that the person who was freed was shaken and tearful and the people who were found guilty were smiling proudly. We held a press conference after the verdict came in. At the end of it I enjoyed thundering, "Wake up, America! Wake up before it's too late!"

*Ben and Bill Coffin (center) at press conference after the conviction.*

We were sentenced to two years in jail and fined five thousand dollars each. We appealed, of course. A year later the Court of Appeals reversed the decisions for some of us and suggested new trials for the others. Dismissal of the indictment against me and Michael Ferber was directed because of lack of evidence of guilt. New trials were ordered for Coffin and Goodman because the questionnaire was considered an interference with the jury's duty to decide on the single conspiracy count. Oddly, during the trial when the issue arose it was Leonard Boudin and Telford Taylor, the constitutional appellate lawyers, rather than the more active trial lawyers, who first objected to the judge's proposal. The reasons were technical: the judge should not have asked for separate verdicts on the three counts.

Before I was indicted, most reporters and interviewers were rather condescending. They took the attitude: "Doctor, presumably you know something about child development, but *what* gives you the idea that you know anything about the war in Vietnam? Don't you know that the president is in immediate communication with the generals in Vietnam at all times, and that he knows exactly what he's doing? What gives you the idea that you might know better than the president what we should be doing?" As I got bolder and the failure of the government's policy was shown up more and more, I was able to say, "Well, how come the president, with all of this input, has proved wrong in every respect about Vietnam? And why is it that the antiwar people have been proved right again and again?" What was interesting—and mysterious—to me was that after the trial and the reversal of the verdict the media dropped their scorn and treated me with a lot more respect about the war.

A couple of weeks after I was indicted, Reverend Norman Vincent Peale preached a sermon at his church in New York City that was reported in a full column in the *New York Times*. He said that all the irresponsibility, the lack of discipline, and the lack of patriotism of young people—by which he meant their opposition to the war—were caused by the fact that when they were babies, their parents followed my advice to give them instant gratification. His accusation caught on with many conservatives. Dozens of conservative newspapers all over the United States printed editorials and columns agreeing with Peale: "That's right—it's Spock who corrupted this whole generation." This accusation cut the sales of *Baby and Child Care* in half for a while, not so much because I was considered a traitor as because the book's advice, it was feared, would produce spoiled brats.

I'm sure that Peale never looked into *Baby and Child Care*. Hundreds of people have told me that they see no instant gratification or permissiveness in the book, that it seems like very sensible and middle-of-the-road advice. But to this day I still get a sprinkling of hate letters saying, "Thank God I never used your horrible book! That's why my children wear clean clothes, take baths, and get good grades in school." It's *always* people who've never used the book who are sure it's permissive and corruptive. To me the best evidence that the accusation grew out of the Vietnam War was that in the previous twenty-two years, since the book's first publication, no one had charged me with permissiveness or advocating instant gratification.

In the congressional elections of 1970, Vice-President Spiro Agnew, campaigning for candidates all over the United States, would tell audiences that I was a corrupter of youth. Opponents of the war in Vietnam, many of them in hippie garb, demonstrated outside the hall during these political rallies and sometimes were invited in by the Republican managers and given special seats in the gallery. Often they would get rowdy, sometimes fairly obscene, and would heckle the speakers, including Agnew. When the heckling became quite noisy, Agnew would interrupt his speech to say, "Look at these youths that Spock has spawned." And all the television cameras would swing around and show them hollering and waving their rude signs. Well, I certainly can't be blamed for Agnew, who was forced to resign from office because of criminal charges against him—he was too old to have been raised by me!

My opposition to the war did cause me one unexpected problem. Early in 1967 I had ordered a new, thirty-five-foot sailboat to live on in retirement. Finally, after a year right after the indictment— it was ready. The builder, Seafarer of Huntington, Long Island was to truck the boat into the Brooklyn docks, where there was a freight line to the Virgin Islands. (There were two other lines: one in Hoboken, the other in Miami.) Somehow the longshoremen found out whose boat it was. Now, the longshoremen of New York take their foreign policy very seriously, which I approve of. They often differ with the government of the United States and sometimes carry out their own foreign policy. They said they refused to load the yacht of a rich traitor. Women Strike for Peace were indignant at this turn of events and were planning to go down to the Brooklyn docks to picket the longshoremen. But that night on television a big, burly longshoreman said, "You know what I'd like to do? I'd like to hoist his boat way, way up and drop it on the dock." I got in touch with Women Strike for Peace and begged them not to ruffle the longshoremen!

The builder agreed to get the boat on a truck again and bring it back to Huntington. Meanwhile their shipping agent got in touch with the freight lines in Hoboken and then in Miami and, without naming any names, asked if they could make room for a thirty-five-foot sailboat going to the Virgin Islands. The same answer came from both lines: "Not if it's Spock's boat!" So I had to engage a man in Larchmont who recruits crews to sail boats here and there. It was no great disadvantage: the price for shipping it on a freighter was about the same as hiring three men to sail it. The builder trucked it to Charleston, South Carolina, where the three men took over and sailed it to the Virgin Islands.

B ILL COFFIN comes from a distinguished old New York family. His mother was a *grande dame*, of the old school, and it must have come as a shock to have her son, the chaplain of Yale University, on public trial for conspiracy. But a stiff upper lip was part of her upbringing, so she came to the courtroom every single day and was very brave about the whole thing.

When the trial was about three-quarters over, the brother-in-law of Jessica Mitford (who was writing a book on the trial) gave a buffet dinner for the five defendants, their families and counsel—some fifteen lawyers—and sympathetic members of the press. We were all having cocktails in the living room when dinner was announced, and I walked into the dining room with Mrs. Coffin. There in the center of the table was the *pièce de résistance*, a huge cold salmon three feet long, coated with glistening mayonnaise. Set into the side, in red peppers, was the Greek letter omega, which in electrical engineering circles stands for resistance and so had been picked up as a symbol by the war resisters. Mrs. Coffin caught sight of it, drew herself up proudly, and said, "At least it's not the hammer and sickle!"

Leonard Boudin is an extraordinary lawyer. He has a worldwide reputation as a constitutional lawyer and has represented the governments of Cuba and Greece in America. He's also a very delightful, sensitive person with a lot of quick wit. He continues to invite us to see him and his wife Jean, a poet, when we are in New York, and he sometimes sails with us in the Caribbean. He used to invite me to play chess with him. I know that he is a good chess player. I've never played chess, and, as I've told him, I have no desire to get involved in such an intricate game with such long pauses between moves. But I love talking with him.

Not long ago Leonard and I were at a fundraising cocktail party and dinner for a peace organization held at Ramsey Clark's apartment in New York. Back at the height of the opposition to the Vietnam War, General Hershey, who was in charge of the draft, complained that he couldn't do his job because so many people were opposing the war and calling it unconstitutional. Ramsey Clark, then the attorney general of the United States, said at the time that he had acted on his own initiative, in response to Hershey's plea, in going after the five of us. But I don't believe that he acted on his own without consulting the president.

At this fundraiser I was asked to say a few words. I said it was exciting to be in the company of both the man who had indicted me for conspiracy and the man who had defended me against those charges. Afterward I felt I had been crude to publicly remind our host that he had tried to throw us in jail. Twice since the end of the Vietnam War, Ramsey Clark has given peace awards to me, among other people, and both times he said, "Spock was right and I was wrong." Not many people who've held public office ever admit to even the smallest mistake. I admire Ramsey Clark for that, as well as for leaving the establishment and becoming a protestor and an attorney for other protestors.

*Leafletting a worker at Seabrook nuclear facility,
in New Hampshire.*

# 18

IN 1972, I FOUND MYSELF the People's Party's candidate for the presidency of the United States. This experience demonstrated the reluctance of the American press and much of the public to see anything in elections except the personalities of the Republican and Democratic candidates and their weekly standing in the polls, as if elections meant nothing more than the World Series or a horse race.

The press treated me with perplexity—"What are you trying to do?" This reminds me of an article Barry Commoner wrote after spending a year as the Citizens' Party candidate in 1980. He found it a galling experience for a variety of reasons, chiefly the lack of understanding by the press. The lowest point in the campaign, he said, came when a puzzled interviewer asked him, "Professor Commoner, are you a serious candidate or are you only interested in the issues?"

When I gave speeches, the main theme was: As you approach an election, there's no point in stewing over which major party you want to vote for, because you get the same imperialist foreign policy and the same unfair domestic policy from both. My speech would last for one hour, followed by another hour of questions and answers where we'd come back again and again to this point about the Democrats being almost as subservient to industry as the Republicans. And invariably, at the end some cheerful-faced undergraduate would come up to the platform and say, "Great speech! You've got me convinced that we need an entirely new economic system. But I can't vote for you, of course, because I'd be wasting my vote." That would undo all my work of the last two hours.

The People's Party was put together in 1971 in a convention assembled by small, independent radical groups in ten states—Vermont, Massachusetts, New York, Pennsylvania, Michigan, Florida, Texas, Arizona, Utah, and California. It was feminist, democratic, and socialist—true equality for women, and similarly oppressed minorities.

First of all, we were against the draft and for rapid, progressive disarmament negotiated with the Soviet Union and other countries. We wanted an end to interference by the U.S. in Third World nations.

We opposed any taxation except a resumption of the progressive income tax, without the loopholes favoring industry and the wealthy. We were most emphatically against property taxes, which are unfair to poorer homeowners and dispose them to vote against increases in school taxes. We were against the sales tax and the Social Security tax, both of which are very regressive. We were for a negative income tax so that everybody would have at least a modest income and anyone who was able to work could keep some of their earnings above the decency level, and thus be encouraged to keep on working. And we were for free university education for anyone who was able to pass entrance examinations.

A very important part of the platform was local political control wherever possible. Needless to say, this did not include foreign policy or the armed forces. But it would be not just municipal control at the municipal level for as many services as possible, it would be neighborhood control. In other words, the people of every neighborhood would, to the greatest practical degree, control police and fire departments, and schooling. After a great deal of anguish and debate, we were in favor of people deciding school policies within their neighborhood, even if this meant certain neighborhoods could ban what they considered—after debate— pornographic literature. The goal was to allow people to have a measure of power and say-so over their lives, particularly blacks, who have felt in many cities that the white board of education and the white schoolteachers maintained discrimination of one kind or another in the schools. They wanted there also to be black principals and teachers. (In New York City this led later to local boards of education.)

The first organizing convention of the People's Party was held in the fall of 1971 in Houston. Some of the figures in it were Marcus Raskin and Gore Vidal. Toward the end it was decided that there was going to be a presidential candidate; I was the favorite, partly because I was well known and partly because I could pay my traveling expenses, but I didn't think I was the ideal candidate— I was already sixty-nine in 1972 and had no background as a radical. But Marcus Raskin and the others were so persuasive in their arguments that I finally agreed. We managed to get on the ballot in only ten states—yet that was no small accomplishment for an independent party, since the ballot laws are designed to discourage independent parties, and balloting officials think of them as a damned nuisance.

My campaign manager was Jim McClellan, one of the key people in getting the People's Party going—a very quiet person, since those days a teacher in a community college in Washington, D.C. He was also part of the Washington office tending to my schedule, not just my itinerary but such practical matters as buying the tickets.

So beginning around January or February 1972 I chased all over those ten states giving speeches. I was on the road for what seemed half my time. This was the period when the hippie mode was much in evidence. Hippies and the People's Party were alike in being concerned with deep issues and uninterested in the conventional niceties. In the apartments where I would be put up for the night there would be clean sheets sometimes, but more often hippies' sheets. Often the washstand wouldn't have been thoroughly cleaned for a long while. Nor the toilet bowl. Four years later Margaret Wright, the 1976 presidential candidate and I were commiserating about what hard work it was to run for president on the People's Party ticket and the kind of places we had had to sleep in. "And Ben," she said, "the *cat hairs* in the bed!"

The cars were battered old hulks, and we had to allow for the possibility that the car meant to take me to a meeting might well refuse to start that morning; another one always had to be lined up. Since these cars were constantly used for political purposes, they were stuffed as much with campaign literature as with old Coke bottles and crumpled beer cans.

I spoke principally on college campuses, where you could always get an audience of several hundred, what with students who were curious, faculty who were liberals, a sprinkling of townspeople, and always an FBI agent, very conspicuous in the middle of the audience in his camel hair coat and felt hat.

In early September the assistant secretary of the Treasury called from the Republican Convention in Miami to say that the secretary had authorized him to offer me Secret Service protection. I said, "You mean a Secret Service man would be with me for two months?" He said, "Twenty-four Secret Service agents!"—three shifts around the clock. Such a possibility had never occurred to me. I don't think any independent candidate had ever been offered it before. Being a good party man, I consulted the Party. The Party said, "Sure, it might give us credibility." And I consulted Jane who said, "It just might keep you from being killed."

Well, it was enjoyable to have lots of company when traveling around. They were a cheerful, witty group of men. When I went to California for two weeks of campaigning, all I had to do was get myself from New York to Los Angeles, where the Secret Service took over with Chrysler limousines. There were always two Secret Service men in my limousine: the driver and one of the inspectors.

My cover name was Randall. That was to fool assassins so that they wouldn't know when the Secret Service was talking about me. I usually traveled with three cars. The lead car would be called "Advance Randall," my car was "Randall," and the car behind us to keep us from being assassinated from the rear was "Randall Follow-Up."

At the time Jane and I were living in an apartment house on East 83rd Street. It was fun when we decided to go shopping. There was one Secret Service man sitting outside our apartment door at all times, even when we were out (in order to keep assassins from inserting themselves into the apartment). We would communicate with the agents by using a white telephone, which connected with the headquarters in the basement and also with the headquarters in a hotel on 86th Street where they all stayed. I would pick up the white telephone, and a voice would say, "Yes, sir," and I would say, "This is Spock, and we want to go shopping. First to Bonwit's and Saks Fifth Avenue and then to Bloomingdale's. We want to leave at ten o'clock," and he would say, "Yes, sir." Promptly at ten o'clock a Secret Service man would come up from the basement, ride down with us on the elevator, and accompany us out the lobby, past the doormen. Back in 1968 when I was under indictment, I'm quite sure the FBI was in constant touch with the doormen to ask who came in to see me, what they looked like, and so on. During that time the doormen were so hostile that they looked the other way when I went through the lobby. Now to have Secret Service swarming all over the place brought them back to respect again, though they must have been puzzled.

There would be three limousines lined up on the street. Jane and I were always meant to sit in the rear, she on the left side and I on the right, so that in case guns went off, the inspector sitting in the right front seat could leap over the back of the seat and land on top of me, sacrificing his own life if necessary.

We would whisk down Fifth Avenue to Bonwit's, and there would be a Secret Service agent standing on the sidewalk to keep a parking space open. It's fun to go shopping under these circum-

stances! One of the men in the front of the limousine would accompany Jane and me into the store, and when Jane would model
a dress for us, he would say, "Very becoming, Mrs. Spock."

Occasionally we would go to a movie (preferably an unusual
foreign movie) or the ballet. They bought their own tickets; I didn't
have to treat them to anything. The Secret Service agents would
position themselves around us so that there would be one on my
right on the aisle, Jane would be on my left, and just beyond Jane
would be another agent. And then behind me would be two more.
Most of them had not been to a weird French or Italian movie or
to the ballet. Their comment would usually be: "Very interesting."

When we were on the road, I let them down with our accom-
modations. The Chrysler limousine would pull up in front of some
rundown house or cheap motel and one or two agents would have
to sit all night long in the front seat and another two would have
to be in the living room and the backyard. And before we would
come into this place, they would have to search it, looking under
the beds, but they never found anything suspicious. When I went
to Party headquarters in Washington, D.C., I would stay at a third-
rate hotel half a block away—respectable enough, but with cracks
in the plaster and paint peeling off the radiator. I had to pay all
my expenses. To them, the worst thing was that they had no television to watch when off duty. In general they were not complainers, but one of them said to me, "Doctor, a block away there's a
much better motel, and it's only a couple bucks more per night,
where they have television." So to be cooperative I went down to
this motel, and of course the nightly rate was two to three times
higher.

They all heard my speech again, again, and again, often three
or four times in one day. They joked that if I ever got sick, any
one of them would be glad to take over and give the speech. When
they had to camouflage themselves in the audience, it was amusing
to see their idea of hippie dress. They simply weren't hippie types,
what with their preference for neat haircuts and clean tweed jackets

*With a young demonstrator at a welfare rights rally,*
*Boston Common, 1967.*

and tan trousers, so they stuck out like sore thumbs. Two or three might be in the front row of the audience, others would be in the back, and I imagine there would be somebody backstage too.

When I was in the Los Angeles area and Jane would be with me, we'd stay with Herb and Shirley Magidson, very good friends from the beginning of the antiwar movement. If anybody in California was in charge of the opposition to the war in Vietnam, it was Herb Magidson. He was a successful manufacturer, specializing in the foam brassieres used in bathing suits; he invented the machinery that turned out the forms that could then be stitched into bathing suits. He lived in a beautiful house in Beverly Hills where the view, particularly at night, was breathtaking, with all of Los Angeles sparkling down below.

One afternoon at five o'clock Jane wanted to know how soon I would be back for dinner. She walked into the bedroom designated as the command post, and asked, "Do you know when Dr. Spock will be back from campaigning this afternoon?" They said "Just a minute," and talked into their walkie-talkie and said, "Two minutes." Jane turned around and walked to the front door and there I was.

On election day I made an appearance at the Bureau of Indian Affairs, in Washington, which had been taken over by the radical American Indian Movement. We wanted to assure them that the People's Party was with them in their protest against many betrayals by the federal government. This proved an embarrassment for the Secret Service, which didn't want to be responsible for protecting me while I was in a government building that had been captured by a rebel group. They feared I might even be taken hostage. So the Secret Service asked me to sign a release from their protection—in quintuplicate. While we were waiting in the limousine for Jim McClellan to arrange for my entrance, the inspector, who had been on the walkie-talkie, joked that "Jim McClellan has been scalped already."

. . .

I GOT seventy-nine thousand votes in those ten states. Multiply eighty thousand by five (we were able to get on the ballot in only a fifth of the states), and we would have got roughly four hundred thousand. That's not impressive, but at least it's visible. Eugene Debs got a million votes at the height of the Socialist vote in America in the 1920s.

The next day I went back to New York and then down to the Virgin Islands. Meanwhile, I'd bid a fond farewell to my Secret Service friends. It felt strange not to have twenty-four people circulating around me, watching me every minute.

*Mary Morgan giving Ben the once over in Little Rock, Arkansas,*
*April 1975.*

# 19

IN 1975 I had been retired from teaching for eight years and had recently separated from Jane. I was living by myself in New York on the third floor of a Madison Avenue brownstone in the eighties, in a one-room so-called studio apartment over a delicatessen.

In April I gave a talk to the Department of Child Development at the University of Arkansas, Little Rock. A member of the audience was Mary Morgan. Coming to hear me was not her idea. A friend of hers who was taking a nursing course had invited her to come along, and Mary had answered that she was not interested in a discussion of child development, since she wasn't having any more babies. Later in the day this nurse came by and offered to cook Mary a spaghetti dinner if she would go to the talk. And Mary said that for a spaghetti dinner, she would go.

A year and a half later, when Mary and I were getting married, a photographer for the *Arkansas Gazette* produced some photographs taken at that first meeting, with me up on the platform after the talk. A dozen or so people always come up to shake hands and ask if I know their Aunt Nelly. Mary was among them—a petite, good-looking woman forty years younger than I. She was looking me over very carefully, first from the front and then from both sides; you could see that she was moving around the platform. She said later that she was not too impressed with the talk, which, as it happened, was not about child development but the need for health insurance—not an exciting topic. She told me, however, that she was impressed by how well I'd handled the questions— and also by how large my hands were. This was the only time I ever made an impression based on the size of my hands.

Mary was a program organizer and had moved to California. On December 4 and 5, 1975, she invited me to San Francisco to speak along with Claude Steiner on the uses and abuses of power. It was most unusual for me, who had done public speaking for many years, to be invited by somebody not connected with an organization such as a university or a peace group. At that time my speeches were being handled by—and my fees were going to—the People's Party. They said they didn't know how financially responsible Mary was. She had offered a good, big fee for a combination of a talk at Glide Memorial Church one evening and then a workshop all the next day. They advised me to make my telephone calls to her collect. Mary says that I would call her collect and then talk and talk, but maybe she's teasing. I thought I was brief on the telephone.

Mary met me at the San Francisco airport with a dozen red roses. At the hundreds of talks I've given, nobody had ever done that. I was in San Francisco primarily to give this talk for her, but I sandwiched in a committee meeting with the Peace and Freedom Party and a visit to the day care center they had organized. I spent the night with some of the Peace and Freedom Party people. Mary told me afterward that she felt jealous having to let go of me so soon after I'd arrived in San Francisco.

The next day I turned up as planned, and Mary took me to breakfast at a restaurant on the oceanfront in San Francisco and told me I could order anything I wanted. So I took advantage of this invitation and ordered steak and eggs. I didn't stop to think that Mary was paying out of her pocket for that luxurious breakfast.

It was a successful speaking weekend. And from the start I felt stirrings of romantic love for Mary. I was attracted by her vivacity, her beauty, and her intense personalness. She was not a person you could possibly ignore in any situation. By the end of the weekend I was falling heavily in love with her and she with me.

I invited Mary to come to New York for a visit in January 1976. By that time I had been separated from Jane for the better part of a year, but very few people besides our own close friends knew. Certainly, it was not public knowledge. I didn't want to start rumors until Mary and I knew each other a lot better. When she came to New York, I hid her; we didn't go out together. But after two or three days I had the idea that we could safely go to the opera because, as I told Mary, I had no friends who were opera-lovers. So we went, and who should we run into at the intermission but Sey Chassler, the editor-in-chief of *Redbook* magazine, for which I had been writing for a dozen years, and his wife: Natalie. I was so flustered that I couldn't remember Mary's name to introduce her and she had to supply it herself. Sey Chassler laughed all the way back to his seat.

On that trip in January Mary had arrived from California wearing warm-weather clothes, and she was shivering. I also thought she must be very self-conscious to be wearing white in winter in New York, but she really didn't care as much as I did about her clothes. Anyway, the first thing we did was to buy her some warm clothes at Gimbels. She was shocked by the rude grabbiness of the customers.

Shortly before our marriage, my son John was driving with Mary from Rogers in northwest Arkansas, where we were building a house, to Little Rock in the center of the state, where the wedding would be. John exclaimed at one point, "Look at that field of white flowers!" Well, the white flowers were cotton, which Mary had picked as a child (just as she and other children had picked strawberries, another big Arkansas crop). She has never since let John or me forget that we were such ignorant Yankees that we didn't even know what cotton looked like in the field.

*Wedding day, October 24, 1976, Little Rock.*

Since my retirement as a professor in 1967, I had spent half my time in the Virgin Islands and on the other boat in Maine. I dearly loved the scene, the cruising, the relaxation, in both places, though I was as busy at sea as on land—writing articles and books, keeping up with correspondence, going out on frequent speaking tours. Mary had had no boating experience when we met, but she took an immediate interest and learned the essentials of sailing in half a day's sail in the Virgin Islands. She learned to row a dinghy adequately within two or three days. Not only that: On her first sail Mary got seasick. When I told her what it was, she said firmly, "I'm not going to be seasick anymore." And she wasn't. Mind over matter.

· · ·

MARY IS BY FAR the person closest to me. When she is away, I miss her and keep looking for her. I was much closer to my mother than to my father. It was a woman teacher, Caroline Zachry, who taught me so much about child development and childhood education. I was selected by a woman principal to be school physician at a girls' school. It was a woman director of maternal and child health who wanted to use my special training in the New York City Health Department. It seems that it has been particularly women who have appreciated what I've had to offer professionally. Socially I respond to women who approve of me. I've never understood how a man could yearn for a woman who was indifferent to him.

Have I been a good husband? Yes and no. I've been a conscientious, responsible husband. I have shared in the housework and child care. I get involved in projects that I think of as being pleasing to Mary (but sometimes I don't consult her, and then I'm very surprised that she doesn't appreciate my efforts in a project that sometimes she never wanted).

Both of my marriages have been affected by conflict between my unconscious desire for a positive, strong woman and my conscious wish for independence. Together, these forces (especially what with Mary being the ball of fire she is) tend to bring about a lot of rivalry—even as to who will raise and lower the sails, do the anchoring, and sail the boat up to the dock, particularly when new guests are aboard. Mary and I are both highly opinionated and controlling people. But she is casual and I am fussy, so it works out differently. I am underassertive in manner but strongly determined underneath. I've disappointed both wives by being relatively unsympathetic to their ailments, having grown up in a family where we were expected to get well as quickly as possible, with no self-pity. Both wives have complained at times that I'm flirtatious, though it doesn't lead anywhere; I feel that they are overly possessive.

Six years ago we began individual analysis, joint therapy, and group therapy in the Virgin Islands with Dr. Michael Woodbury

*Mary Morgan, November 1985, Nicaragua.*

to solve some of the tensions between us. I think most married people have such tensions—some just tend to cover them up. We feel that the analysis has already made our marriage into a much warmer, mutually supportive relationship. The age difference has not been a problem though people seem to expect it to be.

M ARY AND I ENJOY the same kinds of friends. Her women friends are extremely important to her, more than her men friends, and mean more to her than my friends do to me. I don't crave intimacy with other people much of the time, but Mary needs them, and while she's with them she's full of animation and humor.

Mary expects the best from all grandmotherly types. In child-hood she could always count on her paternal grandmother, known as Mom, for understanding and affection. Mary's nuclear family lived with Mom during Mary's pre-school days. Mom was a midwife and raised white-faced cattle in rural Arkansas. She had a wealth

*Mary and Ben aboard* Turtle *in Rockport, Maine.*

of stories to tell, both real and fanciful, about Indians, cardinal birds, and the War Between the States.

So when we sail across Sir Francis Drake Channel in the British Virgin Islands to spend a few days at Peter Island, we usually pick Great Harbor, partly because it's large and well protected and provides good snorkeling (tobacco fish, French angel fish, and Nassau groupers, aside from the common species). But the greatest attraction for Mary is Mme. LaFontaine, a local fisherwoman in her seventies who was born on the island.

Mme. LaFontaine has been a widow for a dozen years and supports herself mainly by netting bonitas in a seine when a school of them comes into the harbor in the late afternoon. She sells them at market Road Town and to the nearby hotel. Sometimes the bonitas stay away for months. And her own helpers don't fish on

*Mike and Judy Spock with Dan (10), Peter (8), and Susannah (2) in Lincoln, Massachusetts, 1969.*

*John Spock and Cindy Kludt aboard Carapace in the British Virgin Islands, March 1988.*

Saturdays, because they are Seventh Day Adventists; or they may come to work late or not at all. But when things are going right, Mme. LaFontaine spots the bonitas thrashing around a quarter of a mile away and moving up into the bay. She calls out orders from the shore as her crew, in an outboard skiff, sets the seine and herds the fish into it, with loud shouting and violent beating of the water—her old dog, Pet, joins in. From the seine the fish are guided into the crawl, where they slowly circle until it is time for them to be taken to market, sold, and eaten.

Mary and Mme. LaFontaine sit for hours down at the bay talking about fish, the olden days and the pirates, the evil scheming of others to get her strategically located strip of land away from her, the thoughtlessness of yachtsmen who anchor too close to her operation and scare the bonitas away. My grandmothers seemed forbidding and this, if anything, prejudiced me against old people,

*John and Cindy's twins, at 7 months.*

though I am old myself. (Incidentally, I dislike euphemisms like "retirees," "senior citizens," and "golden agers." I think it's more respectful of old people to call them old, provided you respect them.)

A LL FOUR of my sisters are still alive. My brother (who died in 1977) and two of my four sisters have been school teachers for at least part of their careers. One sister has been a psychologist and director of guidance clinics; the other has compiled a monumental bibliography on alcoholism.

My older son, Michael, was for twenty-five years a director of the Children's Museum of Boston, where children are encouraged to play with the exhibits. He has recently gone on to the Field Museum in Chicago. His wife, Judy, has been a designer and director of special education projects for school children, and is an active trustee of Antioch College. They have had three children, two boys and a girl.

John, who is eleven years younger than Mike, is an architect and builder in Los Angeles. His wife, Cindy Kludt, trained first as a nurse and later as a psychotherapist. In August 1988, they had twins, a boy and girl—the newest Spocks.

*Ben walks Ginger down the aisle on May 20, 1989.*

# 20

A MAGAZINE ARTICLE I wrote twenty-five years ago on how to be a stepparent had a lot of wisdom in it, I thought. But in 1975, when I actually became a stepfather to Ginger, Mary's eleven-year-old daughter, I found that I didn't know beans about being a stepparent. Or, at least, my miserable feelings wouldn't let me carry out my own suggestions from that long-ago article. I'd had no idea how painful it is to feel rejected by someone within the family or how hard it is to respond rationally to this.

I'll start by declaring that the step-relationship is just naturally accursed, naturally poisonous. It's no accident that so many fairy tales have wicked stepmothers or cruel stepfathers. Stepparents can seem like a threat to the children involved. After all, it isn't the children who fell in love with this outsider or gave this interloper permission to take up half of the true parent's attention. And often the stepparent barges into the family at a time when the children have become unusually close with the parent because of the divorce or the other parent's death. So the stepparent often provokes intense jealousy and resentment. To justify these feelings, the children exaggerate the stepparent's defects and ignore his or her good qualities.

I'm focusing on the negatives, of course. Children are sometimes quite cordial to the stepparent. But beneath the surface the readiness to turn bitter is usually lurking, and may show up as uncooperativeness or rudeness. Sooner or later this gets under the skin of even an understanding and patient stepparent, who eventually gets cross, perhaps openly angry, and starts to act disapproving of the children—who, in turn, see this as proof of hostility and behave worse. The stepparent then is tempted to reproach the parent for having brought up such badly behaved children and asks that they be corrected. The children, therefore, think that the stepparent is trying to turn their parent against them. The unhappy parent feels torn: to make a move either way is certain to hurt and alienate someone.

What I've described is a typical situation. It certainly was mine. Ginger had had her mother pretty much to herself—in the sense of having no serious competitor—from the age of seven, when her parents were divorced, until I stepped in four years later. Mary and I were partly committed to each other before Ginger even had a chance to meet me. From the outset she was robbed of any say-so in her mother's choice. Then Mary and I, in our enthusiasm for each other, gave too little weight to Ginger's feelings. I had never had an adolescent daughter. But I remembered how my sons at that age were only a little less accessible, a little more secretive about their lives and feelings than when they were younger—no real problem.

I was in my seventies, three generations separated from Ginger, but I don't think that was the essence of the problem. And her loud music and her constant telephoning to her friends annoyed me only mildly—we had been careful to build our house with relatively soundproof walls in Ginger's room.

The intensely irritating thing was Ginger's constant appearance of resentment at my presence in the family and her reluctance to communicate with me.

I tried to be understanding and patient. When I didn't succeed, I grew more and more resentful of her apparent rudeness and expressed my frustration by becoming critical: about the mess she left her room in each morning, the way she threw her wet towel and dripping washcloth on top of her soiled clothes, her table manners, her extravagance in shopping at the most expensive stores, the loudness of her radio, her refusal to wear her orthodontic braces. Here I was invading her life and telling her how to live. Intellectually I knew that as a stepparent I should at all costs avoid disciplining, which could only be counterproductive. It gives the child the opening to say, "You're not my parent and I don't have to obey you." But I couldn't follow my own advice; I grew obsessed with trying to make her behave.

For the first three or four years that we shared a home, it seemed to me Ginger rarely looked at me or spoke to me. When I would drive her to school because she'd missed the bus, I would try to make conversation but get no response except for a muttered "Yes" or "No." Once or twice a year I'd explode. "Ginger," I said one day, "in my seventy-five years I've been acquainted with thousands of people, but not one of them has been as rude as you!" I thought I saw a faint smile of triumph. When I pointed out that she never answered my good morning she replied, "I said hello but it was too quiet for you to hear."

I craved sympathy from Mary and wished she would crack down on Ginger's impoliteness. I wanted her to correct the situation by magic. She listened to my complaints but quite properly wanted to avoid appearing to turn against Ginger on the basis of my accusations. She saw better than I how Ginger was suffering. And she pointed out that my two adult sons had not summoned up much graciousness to welcome her into our family, even though *they* were not going to live in the same house with us, or even in the same part of the country. Mary told friends that she felt her arms were being pulled out of their sockets by Ginger and me.

Poor Ginger not only felt a direct threat of having me in her life but got called names by classmates whose parents knew me as a

*Ginger and Mary, 1984.*

liberal or radical in my political views. Ginger was called a communist and a socialist because of me.

After a year of worsening relations, I went to a specialist in stepfamily problems. She couldn't offer me any quick solution—counselors never can. But she helped me a great deal simply by telling me that I had been living in a fool's paradise if I thought I would be accepted by a stepchild within a year or two. (Some stepparents, of course, are a success from the start—and my admiration for their tact and patience is boundless.) To hear that what I was experiencing was to be expected did relieve a lot of my guilt and sense of failure. As a result, I became a bit more patient, and Ginger and I made a gradual peace.

Long after these events, Ginger and I were asked to write companion pieces for *Redbook* and also to appear on a television program. I urged her to write and speak frankly about how she had *felt* and how the relationship had seemed to her at that time, not to try to judge who was at fault or who was right. I said I'd do the same. In describing her side of the relationship, Ginger emphasized how close she and her mother had been since her parents' divorce, what a shock it had been to find that her mother and a man she herself hardly knew seemed to be rapidly heading for marriage, how she feared losing her mother, and how abandoned she felt when her mother went sailing with this man in the Virgin Islands or in Maine.

When she came to describing how she had felt about me and how she had treated me, it sounded like an utterly different relationship from the one I remembered. She denied any recollection of having given me the cold, hostile treatment that I recalled so painfully. She wrote, "I didn't hate him; I was just watching him." If she felt any lack of cordiality at the time, she was sure it lasted only a few months, not years. Her version made me wonder whether, in my misery, I had grossly exaggerated her hostility. When she was asked in the interview what started the improvement, she said it was when I took her side in an argument with her mother. Stepparents should note this.

In any case, the point is that the intrusion of a stepparent can cause enough dismay and resentment to completely blot out reasonableness and politeness. (Could an adult be cordial when confronted with an armed robber in the bedroom?) Sooner or later the child's hostility will get under the stepparent's skin and cause anger, further convincing the child that this is a mean, untrustworthy person.

When you look at the problem from the child's perspective, you can see why, in most cases, she feels deeply threatened. The child feels no bond to this interloper; she is not the one who fell in love with him. Even if the prospective stepfather has attractive qualities, it is hard for the child to see and appreciate these, because he is, before all else, an outsider who is claiming a great deal of her mother's attention and affection.

The intensity of this hostility toward the intruder is similar to the jealousy an older child, especially a first child, feels toward a new baby. I've seen a secure, happy, loving child of two years turn bitter, destructive, and cruel.

In retrospect it is clear to me that no matter how much I was suffering, Ginger was suffering more. But at that time I was so

*Ginger Councille, age 18.*

resentful of her attitude toward me that I didn't have room in my heart to feel much sympathy for her. I suspect that part of my resentment came from the fact that this was not an adult but just a little girl who seemed to feel fully entitled to make me miserable for years, and that I was utterly helpless to change the situation.

In the thirteen years I have been in the family, Ginger's and my relationship has very gradually but thoroughly improved. My greatest triumph came when she recommended me as commencement speaker at her high-school graduation and I was able, by speaking scornfully about grades, to gain the favor of the class (at the expense of some faculty disapproval). Now we are good and affectionate friends.

Ginger recently miffed Mary by asking me to walk her down the aisle and give her away at her wedding. As Mary said rightly, "Listen, I carried you, I birthed you, I raised you. Ben had nothing to do with this and you're not going to brush me off this way. How can Ben give you away? You're not his to give!" On May 20, 1989, I walked Ginger down the aisle, then both Mary and I escorted her to the altar to give her away. Before I left her side I whispered, "Okay, kid, you're on your own!"

*Whooping it up with a child before becoming an opponent of war toys.*

# 21

I'VE BEEN ASKED a thousand times: Have I ever changed my advice on child rearing? The answer is no, at least not about my basic belief that it is wise to respect children, but also not to forget to ask respect from them. Contrary to my reputation for permissiveness, I've always urged parents to ask for cooperation and politeness (and to render it to children as well). In *Baby and Child Care*, from the start I've tried to give as little arbitrary advice per se as possible. I try to explain what children are like, what their motives are, their fears, why they act certain ways at certain ages, so that parents will first of all have some idea why a child often behaves contrary to the parents' wishes. I may suggest one or two ways to handle a situation, and with this in mind parents can decide for themselves what to do. That's not the same as telling them just what to do. Most parents who have told me they liked the book have said how they appreciated my leaving decisions to them.

I try to give readers confidence by reminding them they already know a lot, and that the professionals don't know everything. I sympathize. I try not to be pompous and I bend over backward to reassure parents, not to frighten or scold them. This, I think, is the main reason the book has been popular.

Of course, I've changed my mind about small and medium matters and revised the book to reflect the changes. I've changed my mind about toilet training several times and about circumcision. I've also changed my mind somewhat—or at least tried to—about fresh air.

I was brought up with a very strong emphasis on fresh air. By the time I was practicing pediatrics, it was no longer a matter of great pediatric concern, so I tried to reduce its importance in my mind and in my book, but I found I was unable to leave it out altogether. In the first editions of *Baby and Child Care* I urged mothers to get the baby out for a couple of hours in the morning and an hour in the afternoon. I was still living and thinking in terms of New York (and New York's climate). When I went to Rochester, Minnesota, in 1947, I was amazed and rather horrified to see that no babies or young children were taken out in wintertime there. Everybody assumed that it was crazy to expose them to the painfully cold air. I've laughed about my persistent compulsion ever since. Now I say fresh air is a good idea for pepping up appetite and putting pink in the cheeks, especially in winter. So I say get children out of the hot house or apartment, but I'm not fanatical about it.

My ideas on toilet training changed three or four times, reflected in different revisions of the book, and I wound up eventually doing a complete about-face, thanks to the observations of T. Berry Brazelton, a distinguished pediatric researcher from Children's Memorial Hospital in Boston, who has much the same philosophy as mine.

At the time I started pediatric practice, there was a great deal of enthusiasm, especially among college-educated mothers, for early toilet training. This followed the English tradition. English nannies and the earlier English books on raising children emphasized that for the child's health it was extremely important to have a movement every day and at the same hour. This habit was to be instilled during the first year of life by holding the baby on a pot at the time of day when the movement was likely to come. Then, by conditioned reflex, upon feeling the rim of the pot, the baby would strain a little and have a movement. The whole thing would be accomplished and the child set on the royal road to health before the age of a year.

In my psychoanalytic training I learned that Freud and Karl Abraham and other analysts had believed that the origins of compulsive neuroses could be traced in part to overly severe and too early potty training. The child by one and a half or two years resented this external control and rebelled. The parents would intensify their efforts. After a prolonged conflict the child might suppress this rebelliousness and come around to taking the meticulous moving of his bowels to be as important as the parents thought it was.

My wife Jane told me that in Central Park two mothers' conversation might go like this: Mother A would say, "My baby was trained to the potty by six months of age," and Mother B would say, "Well, *my* baby hasn't had a dirty diaper since the age of three months." I was looking for a way to avoid the battles that some parents got into with their children. I asked my psychoanalytic mentors and colleagues what the right age is to start. They could only shrug their shoulders. They may have analyzed the connection between training and neurosis in some of their adult patients, but they were not in a position to turn it around and say just how a neurosis could have been avoided.

When I started pediatric practice, I said to myself, Let's assume that under the age of a year is too early—you would have to be too attentive and too controlling. A year and a quarter, I suggested, was a more wholesome age. I wasn't long in practice before some mothers told me that they had run into great resistance soon after starting. After a while I came to realize that this is just the age

*Ben composed practically everything he's ever written at this drafting table.*

when a baby begins to want to control his own movements—when he is becoming aware of himself as an individual and doesn't want to be dominated in any respect. I had picked a particularly bad age. Soon I shifted it to later in the second year.

My advice in the first edition of *Baby and Child Care* (1946) was based on a discovery made independently by two mothers who had told me essentially the same story. They had gone at their first couple of children's potty training with hammer and tongs, believing it was very important to get them trained early. They ran into a lot of resistance. By the time their third child came along, both of these mothers had been so frustrated by toilet training that they just kept postponing it. To their amazement, one day around two and a half years of age the child, imitating the older children, decided to use either the toilet or the toidy seat and took great pride in being able to do this. The child was trained for bowel movements and urine at about the same time and never regressed.

This is the answer, I thought. And in the first edition of *Baby and Child Care* I suggested: Let the child see another sibling or friend or the parents on the toilet, and the child will want to imitate them. Several mothers wrote to me that they had tried this method of just waiting, and now at two and a half or three years the child showed no sign of training. I realized there was no sure magic in that method. In later editions I suggested being more positive. First let the child see siblings, friends, parents, and then you take control and suggest that the child try it. If the child doesn't get the idea or doesn't seem to take to it, then suggest that the child sit down. If the child wants to jump back up right away, suggest that the child stay a little while. But don't be bossy.

Enough mothers wrote to me or told me that this didn't work either. I realized that I still didn't have the perfect formula. When I got to Western Reserve in Cleveland and was closely associated with the child therapists there, most of whom had been trained by Anna Freud, I found they believed that when the child had reached one and a half or two years of age, the parent should be quite positive about it. I modified my advice accordingly: Suggest firmly that the child sit on the toilet at the likely time of day, and try to keep the child there with firm directions.

Then came Berry Brazelton, who in May 1973 wrote in *Redbook* magazine that in his practice of pediatrics he had used the following method on fifteen hundred babies consecutively: Wait first until the child is interested in containers. Babies between the ages of sixteen months and two years certainly get interested in putting small things into big containers and trying to put big things into small containers. His second step was to get a toidy seat and keep the lid on it so the big hole does not show. Let the child think of it as his own little seat near the floor. Let him play with it, sit on it, feel familiar and friendly with it. In other words, there is no requirement, just a possession that he can be proud of. After he has gotten to feel possessive and friendly toward the toidy seat, then you can suggest, while raising the lid and putting a potty inside, that this also is a toilet he can use for his bowel movement— just as the parent uses the big toilet. But Brazelton emphasized that there is still to be no pressure. If the child doesn't want to sit on it, the parent shouldn't urge. There should be no suggestion that the parents are trying to get the bowel movement away from the child. And he stressed that if the child sits down and then becomes quickly impatient and wants to jump up again, the parents shouldn't try to make the child sit again but wait. No pressure at all. He said that of fifteen hundred babies somewhere between the ages of two and a quarter and two and three-quarters, an overwhelming majority more or less trained themselves, not only for bowel movements but also for urine, at about the same time.

What impressed me most of all was that in these fifteen hundred cases, he said, there were remarkably few who remained bed wetters. This suggested that delayed bed-wetting—a complicated symptom—means that in the beginning the child is protesting against parental overcontrol of bowel movements and perhaps urine in the daytime. This theory is consistent with the very high rate of Englishmen rejected for army service because of bed-wetting. Most bed-wetting, if it becomes established at age three or four years, will last until adolescence.

In the next edition of *Baby and Child Care* (1976) I just borrowed Berry Brazelton's idea and ascribed it to him. But it left a question in my mind: Why, since I had started way back in the thirties with a somewhat similar idea of letting children train themselves by imitation, didn't it seem to work for me? Why did it work for Berry Brazelton in the fifties, sixties, and seventies? He suggested that back in the thirties few parents were willing to wait until age two and a half for success; perhaps they bossed just enough to create resistance.

I N THE FORTIES, I was a sexist like almost everybody else. When the women's liberation movement became active in 1969 and '70, it still took me a long time to acknowledge my own sexism and try to change my ideas. While I was attacking the war in Vietnam, I was being attacked by feminists on the rampage. I was no more sexist than the average man, I think, but since I'd written down so much, the feminists were able to put their finger on it.

At two universities in the early seventies, while I was trying to make anti–Vietnam War speeches, groups of young women students interrupted me with organized demonstrations in which they stampeded in and out of the hall chanting derisively in unison excerpts from my writings. This electrified the audiences and undermined my talks.

In 1972 when I was running for president, I was asked, like all presidential candidates that year, to explain to the National Women's Political Caucus my own views and those of the party in regard to the women's liberation movement and to sexism in general. I realized that it would be a very hostile audience. I entered the hall and sat in the back while Eugene McCarthy gave his speech. Two women came up to me and said angrily, "You'd better get out. You're not wanted here!" I said I'd been asked to come and explain the People's Party position which was emphatically feminist and couldn't just run away. When I got up to speak, several women left the hall. Rather than start by explaining the People's Party point of view, I said, "I want to apologize first for some of the foolish things that I've written and said," then went on to explain the position of the party.

When I finished, Gloria Steinem, who was in the middle of the audience, stood up and thundered in the tones of Jehovah, "Dr. Spock, I hope you realize you have been a major oppressor of women in the same category as Sigmund Freud!" Freud had been very much a Victorian sexist, but that didn't mean he hadn't made profound discoveries about the psyche. So I comforted myself by thinking of it as a compliment, though Steinem didn't mean it as such. *Time* magazine reported, "Spock hung his head in shame." Not exactly in shame. When somebody asks me a hard question in the presence of an audience, I can't answer if I'm looking right at the person. I was looking down at the lectern thinking, What can I say, what can I say? I couldn't think of anything. My instinct to say nothing was probably a good one.

But an apology wasn't enough. Some things in *Baby and Child Care* were obviously sexist. When I wrote that a father's influence on his daughter is no less important than his influence on his son, I gave two examples: that he should compliment his little daughter on the pretty dress she is wearing or on the cookies she has baked. I couldn't have picked worse examples!

It hurt my feelings to be called an enemy of women, after so many women had called me friend and helper. But it is indicative of my sexism that it took me three years of discussions with many patient women before I fully understood the nature of my sexism and felt ready to begin, in 1973, the revision of *Baby and Child Care* that was published in 1976. I had to change every pronoun in the book. I went on to discuss how mothers and fathers can minimize sexism in raising their sons and daughters in our sexist society.

Today I think I've gotten rid of nine-tenths of my sexism. I was delighted when Gloria Steinem and the board appointed me one of the heroes of the women's movement during *Ms.* magazine's tenth anniversary. I'm not saying there's no trace left—my wife Mary has some reservations . . .


AROUND 1980, I began thinking about choosing an editorial collaborator and eventual inheritor for *Baby and Child Care*. I went at it systematically, writing to three professors with philosophies similar to mine—Berry Brazelton, Lewis Fraad, and David

Friedman—asking for names of pediatricians who were psycholog-ically oriented and might be interested in writing for parents. The fifteen people whose names I got I asked to write a couple of pages of advice to parents on a pediatric problem like bed-wetting. Of the eight who responded, I found I liked the writing of four very well. I interviewed them with Mary Morgan, who would be the executor of my estate, and at that point she suggested the name of Michael Rothenberg.

Michael Rothenberg, now coauthor of *Baby and Child Care* and the person who will take it over someday, is a pediatrician and child psychiatrist from the University of Washington in Seattle. Mary had struck up a correspondence with him on the subject of television violence, on which he had earlier testified before a congressional committee and had published a paper that impressed Mary a great deal. I wrote to him, and he responded with a paper within a few days—something that impressed *me* a great deal.

He too believes that the psychological side of pediatrics is as important as the physical. He has great respect for children and parents. He sees that some of the biggest current issues for child care are political questions: We need more high-quality day care and more high-quality schools, better housing, better social ser-vices for deprived children, more money for school lunches and food stamps, good television programs for children, nuclear dis-armament. How do we get them? Political activity—for parents and professionals both.

Michael's testimony before a congressional committee taught me that by the time a kid graduates from high school, he or she has observed eighteen thousand murders on TV. This is a horrible figure when you combine it with findings that every time a child or adult watches brutality on television or on film, he or she is brutalized at least to a slight degree. Multiply that slight degree by eighteen thousand and you've done a lot of harm. Not enough to turn a sensitively brought up child into a thug; but slowly moving everybody—adults as well as children—in the direction of bru-tality.

*Mary, Ben, Michael, and Jo Rothenberg.*

We divided the topics to be revised and then exchanged our parts for each other's suggestions. The closest we came to a difference of opinion centered on my saying in an earlier edition of *Baby and Child Care* that plump babies are much more likely to have severe eczema than skinny babies. He said that he had never heard of this. Neither had a dermatologist and an allergist he consulted in Seattle. But I knew I had gotten it from some authoritative source. I found it in my copy of Henry Holt's textbook of pediatrics, which I'd used in medical school. We compromised by saying, "Some pediatricians believe that plump babies are more likely to have eczema." Thanks to Michael the book ended up with a number of new topics, such as fathers' participation in childbirth, home deliveries, and midwifery.

Most remarkable of all, no signs of crankiness or rivalry developed during our two years of revising. I thought we might clash because I, as the original author, might become bossy and possessive. Yet Michael was no spring chicken. He had been a professor for a long time, and had broad experience. There was no reason for him to defer to me, and he didn't.

Though I still hope to live at least to one hundred, I can die in peace at any time as far as the future of *Baby and Child Care* is concerned.

*A 4-year-old demands, "If you're the real Dr. Spock, where's your space ship?"*

# 22

A FEW YEARS AGO the federal government, under President
Ford, provided free flu shots, particularly for older people,
who are more likely to die of flu. A number of older people promptly
died after taking the shot. As other old people heard about this,
quite a few decided to take their chances with the flu instead.
When I read this in the newspaper, I said, "Well, if I were old, I
would decline to take the flu shot too." I was eighty at the time.

I used to think that when people get old, they all feel they are
turning into another kind of person. But a book I read on the
attitudes of aging people says that they don't think any differently
of themselves as they get older—their sense of identity remains
the same. So it's not unique to me.

I think my impatience with some old people comes from their
having become timid, cautious, anxious, and politically more conservative. I want to be around lively people. I like a restaurant
that's boisterous with laughing and talking and arguing, and I dislike
a restaurant where people are whispering.

Though I'm politically as radical as ever, I continue to be concerned about my appearance. I'm against clothes that are too in-

formal for the occasion, on me or on anyone else. I could never give a talk with my shirt open at the collar and no tie. I have relaxed enough to wear a blazer and a pair of slacks when I speak in California. But I'll wear a three-piece suit if I'm speaking in New York, Boston, or Washington. I would lose conviction in my talk if I thought I was improperly dressed. I still want to dress like Mr. Babcock at Hamden Hall.

I'm going to keep sailing as long as I can clamber aboard a boat. Already I have to be much more careful. It makes me not only nervous but envious to see young people jumping off a float into a dinghy, sure that their coordination will keep them from falling in. I have to kneel down and crawl into a dinghy, because I can't count on my reflexes. It's undignified, ignominious—to be crawling when others are running and jumping. As I go forward to do the anchoring, I hold on to the boom, then the mast, then the forward stays, then the lifelines. I might reach a stage when sailing will seem too dangerous or make me feel uncomfortable, though I can't imagine it. Mary has bought me a special life jacket, but I still refuse to put it on.

Right now we live only on boats, sailing in Maine in summer and in the Virgin Islands the rest of the year. If we decided to live in California, I would want a house. It could be small, though not crowded shoulder to shoulder with other bungalows, as in the built-up parts of California; I'd want to be off by myself. I imagine that the time will come when it's not practical for me to live on boats. But I'll cross that bridge when I come to it. Deny and delay— that's my philosophy!

BEING IN GOOD HEALTH and of sound mind, except for absentmindedness and a wretched memory for names, I don't expect to die for a long time yet. But here in my eighties I'd like to give my relatives some guidelines. As far as I know—and one never knows for sure until the time comes—I don't fear dying itself, as long as it's not very painful or lacking in dignity. But the fear of senility is truly powerful.

A close friend and wise colleague of mine (not a physician) died slowly and painfully of inoperable cancer. She was the sole support of three young children and should have been making plans for their future and discussing these with them. But she never asked anyone for a diagnosis. And nobody, respecting her apparent wish to remain in ignorance, ever volunteered the information. Each time I visited, I expected her finally to ask, and each time I was flabbergasted that she did not. Now, years later, I realize that she might have preferred a frank discussion with her doctor but had been put off by his seeming reluctance to raise the issue.

In those circumstances I would want my physician and my spouse to be honest and cheerful but not to pretend that everything was lovely. I don't want to be surrounded by solemn, whispering tiptoers, but I also don't want hearty, loud-voiced types asking me perfunctorily how I feel or if there's anything I need. I want people who will look me in the eye in a friendly or even loving manner, discuss openly any of my concerns, and ask only those questions which apply to my actual situation.

I would want to take any treatment that had a chance of curing me or keeping me alive and active for a number of years. But I would not want to be kept alive with antibiotics, infusions, transfusions, anticancer drugs, or radiation if they were just to postpone my death for a few months. Especially if I had lost my marbles. Having been brought up with a strong emphasis on appearances, I have a real dread of going visibly senile without realizing it.

Some years ago I happened to be going down in a Plaza Hotel elevator with a famous architect. Though old, he still maintained a dashing appearance: a broad-brimmed, flat-topped cowboy hat such as Gary Cooper wore in *High Noon*, an expensive-looking suit, and a flowing silk bowtie. His jacket, however, was spotted with food. He seemed carefree, but I felt deeply embarrassed for him. Each morning since then I've inspected my jacket carefully,

*Mary and Ben in St. Thomas.*

though I realize that if senility sets in I will have forgotten this precaution.

Of course, the reason why physicians often go to such extremes to keep a hopelessly ill patient alive is that their job, their training, and their ethics direct them to do so. Besides, they can be sued by a disgruntled relative for not having done everything conceivable to prolong the patient's life. When I wonder what directions to leave, I realize that, in addition to my own wishes, there will be Mary's feelings and my doctor's ethics to consider. Even though I've decided in advance that I will choose a planned, peaceful death over unbearable pain, will my doctor be willing to administer the necessary dose of medicine—or to leave it handy—and will Mary have the nerve to jab the needle?

The omission of artificial life support systems is only one aspect of being allowed to die naturally. I would want to be at home, if that wasn't too burdensome, or in a hospice, rather than a hospital. I have been a frequent patient in hospitals, and I am grateful to have had excellent care in all respects. But hospitals are nothing like home. They are more like factories: clean, modern factories for producing diagnoses and treatments. A stream of skilled staffers barges in, as if from outer space: history takers, physical examiners, temperature and pulse takers, meal servers, bath givers, stretcher pushers, X-ray technicians, bed makers, pill pushers, specimen takers, attending physicians, residents, interns, registered nurses, practical nurses, some of them showing no interest in the patient aside from the accomplishment of their particular errand.

In recent years the hospice movement, which began in England, has spread over the U.S. The aim is to let the person die as pleasantly as possible in a homelike setting, surrounded by family and some familiar possessions, and spared pain by regular, heavy medication—without any fussing that is not provided solely for comfort. That's the departure for me.

I dislike intensely the atmosphere of the conventional funeral: the darkened room, the solemn people, silent or whispering or sniffling, the funeral director's assistants pretending to feel mournful. My ideal would be the New Orleans black funeral, in which friends snake-dance through the streets to the music of a jazz band. A satisfactory compromise would be a church service for my friends to think of me together for an hour and say farewell. But I would like them to be normally noisy and cheerful. The music might be the ragtime and jazz I love dancing to because it liberates me from my puritanical upbringing, but also lively hymns and such songs as "The Battle Hymn of the Republic" and "America the Beautiful," which always choke me up, not with sorrow but with exultation. I'd like the service for the dead to be delivered in the rich cadences that have come down to us through the centuries. I'd like the minister—preferably William Sloane Coffin, Jr., who so enjoys life and with whom I was put on trial for our opposition to the Vietnam War—to speak of our hope that the peacemakers really will prevail.

And some child development person or parent could speak of my belief in the potentialities of children and of my agreement with Jesus's words: "Suffer little children, and forbid them not, to come unto me: for of such is the kingdom of heaven."

Followed by a cheerful cocktail party somewhere nearby.

TO WHAT DO I ASCRIBE my longevity? The most likely thing, it seems to me, is the genetic inheritance from my mother. My father died before sixty, and I think so did his father, but my mother and those of her siblings who avoided cancer lived into their late eighties or early nineties. My mother was ninety-one, so obviously I take after her—as do all four of my sisters, who are all still living. (My brother Bob died of a coronary attack at sixty. Single men tend to die young.) My cardiologist tells me I have better than average immunity to arteriosclerosis. That's nothing I can take credit for. It's the genes that my mother gave me.

Some doctors neglect their health by ignoring their own symptoms; for the same reasons, others become hypochondriacs. I'm smug that I've shown good judgment in the many medical and surgical conditions I've had throughout my life: I haven't neglected the symptoms of anything serious, nor have I gone running to doctors for nothing.

I continue to row when I have the opportunity. Two years ago I was in a dinghy race in Tortola that went four and a half miles across Sir Francis Drake Channel. I came in eighth out of eleven entries. I thought I was lucky to finish at all, even luckier not to be the last. Except that I did have a slight advantage that wasn't recognized at the time: my dinghy rowed easier than most of the others competing.

Mary and I meditate twice a day, and I assume that contributes to my well-being. It's probably more helpful that I've avoided eggs for most of the last twenty years. Occasionally I'll go on a bust and have eggs benedict or fried eggs; I agree with E. B. White when

*Climbing up the dock at low water in Cutler, Maine.*

he said, "I love the taste of cholesterol." Mary has become increasingly vegetarian, but she provides fish plentifully and chicken
occasionally, and I eat meat in restaurants. I also take a large daily
dose of vitamins that she prescribes, and only complain a little
about this.

*Opposing missile testing at Cape Canaveral, January 17, 1986.*

# 23

A CHILD TODAY is subject to far more tensions than when I was growing up. More emphasis, proportionately, was placed then on physical health—hence my mother's concern with the right (and wrong) vegetables and fresh air—and on moral character, particularly in sexual matters. Now there is a much higher incidence of both parents working outside the home, more divorce, more single-parent and stepfamilies, excessive competition and materialism, less job satisfaction, the drug scene, more violence of every kind, the fear of nuclear destruction . . . all of these take their toll on parents and children alike. And, of course, these tensions do not replace but compound the inevitable conflicts between children and parents (whatever their convictions) and among siblings, which seem to be inherent in the species. Increasingly, young people are growing up insecure, cynical, desperate for something to believe in, depressed often to the point of suicide, and doubtful whether there may be a future at all.

.   .   .

WHEN I TELL TALES about my childhood, it may often seem quite grim, but I don't think I'm angry anymore. Some people stay angry with their parents through adulthood, still feeling like helpless children deep inside. The normal course of maturity should put an end to such resentment, even though getting angry in the first place was normal. All adolescents grow critical and impatient with their parents to some degree. This is nature's way of dislodging children from their families. If we all continued to feel entirely comfortable within our parents' homes, there would be every reason to stay there forever and none to go out and make a life for ourselves. This impatience is also closely linked to the way progress is made in the culture: dissatisfaction with what already exists in science, technology, all the arts. And, for that matter, with existing political structures and the way a country is being run.

I understand now that my mother's strictness came out of her unusually difficult childhood. I think I see what she was trying to accomplish: she firmly believed that humans are perfectible, if firmly guided, and she never gave up trying to perfect us. As I progressed through adulthood, I realized what strong positive values our parents had given the six of us, and not just by word but by example: courage, idealism, sticking to principle. These served me well, up through the years that led to the writing of *Baby and Child Care* and, beyond that, into the political activism for disarmament and peace which people considered wrongheaded.

I wrote *Baby and Child Care* to tell parents about children, to give them confidence, and to keep them from being intimidated by relatives and professionals. That's why I start right off saying "You know more than you think you do." It hasn't solved the problems of the world—that's for sure—but it has helped parents to steer between timidity and intimidation, which seems to be the trickiest problem for many today.

Another broad aim has been to help parents to respect their children, but—equally important and often forgotten today—to ask for respect from them, to ask for cooperation and politeness.

*Ben with Daniel Ortega, Managua, Nicaragua, 1984.*

What's been the longterm effect of the book? Well, I've been blamed and thanked for all manner of things. I never planned or inaugurated a new generation of young people. I was only helping parents. But I was delighted by what young people did in the sixties in protesting against discrimination, against the war in Vietnam, and against antiquated rules in the universities. I wouldn't call it a "permissive" generation—parents weren't suddenly letting their children do these things, let alone encouraging them—but it certainly was a generation of young people who weren't afraid to come to their own opinions and take the consequences. We need more of that kind of initiative and responsibility today, in a country with so many serious problems.

By and large, it seems to me, this is a materialistic country. It turns to questioning and idealism only when people, especially the young, are aroused by dramatic issues. The twenties, when I was a youth, were strongly materialistic times, and politics were conservative. The Great Depression shook many people's faith in the economic system and made them search for alternatives. After World War II came the reactionary and materialistic late forties and fifties. Civil rights and Vietnam provoked the idealistic fervor of the sixties and early seventies. This was followed in turn by the intense self-absorption and materialism of the mid-seventies and eighties. The youth in each of these contrasting eras must have been of the same stuff. It was the times, the current issues, that brought out their different attitudes. I applauded the rebels of the sixties. They gave me great hope—just as the abrupt relapse right after the end of the Vietnam War hit me in the face like a bucketful of ice water. What will it take to generate the next wave of idealism?

INTERVIEWERS ASK ME what I want to be remembered for. In a sense, that question is already decided: *Baby and Child Care* has been translated into thirty-nine languages and bought by thirty-seven million parents. Although I'd like to be remembered for both the book and for working toward disarmament and peace, my guess is that *far* fewer people will appreciate my peace work or even have heard of it. Some who like the book disapprove of the politics or think that a professional person should steer clear of politics because it's dirty. But I don't want to choose. Disarmament is part of child care, not only in avoiding annihilation but in freeing up money for facilities for children—and their parents.

I believe that if the nations of the world—especially the USSR and the USA—were to take truly significant steps toward disarmament, it would be the greatest possible boon to humanity. I don't want to disparage past disarmament agreements, but they've covered little ground and left loopholes; generally, they've just limited certain types of arms in the future rather than committing the parties to progressive elimination of huge existing stockpiles.

It's tough to get the government to disarm at all. Enormous power is combined in the arms industries, the Congressmen who foster them in their districts, the labor unions, the local media,

*Helen Caldicott, Mary, Bella Abzug, and Ben demonstrating after Three Mile Island.*

the Pentagon—and finally the president, who imagines he is at his most magnificent when threatening to slay the dragon of communism. Disarmament can be accomplished, I believe, if enough people apply pressure. Americans will rouse themselves by the millions to write letters and lobby against tax increases, for instance, when they feel that the government is intruding in their affairs. But they tend to resist even thinking about nuclear weaponry and warfare. Some are so scared by these issues that they shut them out of their minds. Others feel that the issues are too complex— all those kinds of missiles!—and that this is the government's business anyway. Then there is the position that politicians, the press, the Pentagon, and the arms industries have been foisting on the American people for the last seventy years: that we would be selling out to the Russians, or at least lowering our guard, by agreeing to disarm, and that if we became too active we might be accused of being a communist.

We squander trillions of dollars on arms while cutting back on

*Climbing the fence at Cape Canaveral, 1986.*

services for the young, the sick, the poor, and the elderly. Day care is grossly inadequate, and needs subsidies. The quality of schools for most children is poor and unchallenging. The health of future generations depends on good housing, safe neighborhoods, and good medical care for everybody. America has plenty of money for these things, but the only way to make the government spend it in the right ways—and to make it give up its suspicious and belligerent attitude toward the rest of the world—is for citizens to take action. Every effort made in this direction, every letter and every demonstration, has done some positive good. Without these protests, things would be much worse.

Not many people see why civil disobedience is logical or right. For myself I will say that if I have used all legal means—voting, lobbying, letter writing, demonstrating—to influence my government and fellow citizens, and still believe that the government is on a criminal course, I'll participate again in nonviolent civil disobedience. Such an act will get ten times the coverage from television and the press as a legal demonstration, and my discomfort or fine will be a small price to pay. So, every couple of years, I respond to a call from a peace or humanitarian organization, knowing that the older I get, the *more* attention I'll draw to the cause. Especially if there is a barbed-wire fence to be climbed. I'm going to keep climbing until I keel over.

# Acknowledgments

I ONCE HEARD that a deadline is when a publisher falls over dead because the manuscript came in on time. This one was always on time, and there are a number of people to thank for helping make that possible.

I'm most grateful to our secretary, Lynda Long, who didn't walk off and leave us in the middle of this mess. Instead, she gave up evenings and weekends and holidays to transcribe, type, collate, photocopy, package, keep track of things, and see that they actually got where they were headed, and on time. And to demonstrate her devotion, she gave us not just herself but her mother—as Lynda found her responsibilities growing, Louise Young pitched in for long hours at the transcribing machine. My thanks also to those from outside our regular office staff who helped type: Angeline Williams, Sherwin Schulterbrandt, Lori Grooms, Corine Gibson, Eugene Covey, Eric Allen and particularly Berinice Mercer, for her loving support.

A number of people helped transport this manuscript back and forth across the Caribbean seas. We often work while anchored aboard our boat *Carapace* in Great Harbor on Peter Island, in the

ACKNOWLEDGMENTS

British Virgin Islands. Early in the morning I would dinghy over to ask the advice of Mme. LaFontaine, the only fisherwoman in the British Virgins today, and to me an inspiring figure. It was from her harbor that the manuscript would set out, on the Peter Island ferry, and travel across the Sir Francis Drake Channel, where it would be met by Steve Marsh of Caribbean Sailing Yachts. Elmore Woodley would drive the manuscript across Tortola to the West End dock, and Captain Elvin Stout ("Skinny") of the *Native Son* ferry would sail it down to Charlotte Amalie, on the U.S. island of St. Thomas. There Louise would meet it and guide it through U.S. Customs and Immigration, then walk it to our office in Palm Passage, where Lynda would type, copy, and wrap it up for the 3:00 P.M. Federal Express deadline to New York. We kept Federal Express *very* busy. Never once did any of these people let me down, and I have promised each one the first copy.

I want to thank all of the people who kept *Carapace* afloat while we were doing this book. There is Ashton McCall, the mechanic; Steve Marsh, the rigger; Radford Potter, the electrician; Rose Douglas, who purchased supplies, organized, and cleaned; Meyers, the sailmaker; and Elmore Woodley, who took care of the dockage and transportation. Since the book was born on this boat, it couldn't have happened without them. My thanks also to Wayfarer Marine for their care of *Turtle*, our boat in Maine.

And I want to thank my support groups in St. Thomas, Tortola, and Puerto Rico, who help keep *me* afloat.

Judith Viorst's words "You can do it" gave me the confidence to undertake this book, and her loving, never-tiring encouragement and comfort saw me through my later moments of doubt. She has always taken time out of her busy schedule to edit whatever I've sent her, letting me know that I am worthy. Thank you, Judy. You are my model and inspiration.

My special thanks to Bob Lescher, my agent, who was always available to get me through the rough times. Ed Copeland and Leonard Boudin, our lawyers, provided us with sound legal advice and support, as they have done all the time we've known each other.

One of the pleasures of doing this book was working with Doug Woodyard. His sensitive, unobtrusive copyediting makes things clear, and I trust him. Every writer should be blessed with a copyeditor like Doug.

The past six years of individual analysis and joint therapy that Ben and I have taken with Dr. Michael Woodbury have had a profoundly beneficial effect on our life together and on the writing of this book. My respect for Mike goes as deep as my gratitude for our work with him.

And my thanks go especially to Ben, who devoted hours of his own writing and sailing time to answer endless probing questions. He gave his words, his energy, his spirit to this book. I feel honored and privileged to be sharing my life with him.

*Mary Morgan*
*Tortola*
*British Virgin Islands*
*1989*

# PERMISSION ACKNOWLEDGMENTS

"I Didn't Know How to Be a Stepfather" by Benjamin Spock, M.D., originally appeared in *Redbook* magazine, September 1985.

"The Mother's Boy and the New Coach" by Benjamin Spock, M.D., originally appeared in *My Harvard, My Yale*, edited by Diana Dubois, which Random House, Inc., published in 1982. Copyright © 1982 by Benjamin Spock, M.D.

"Two Perspectives on Stepparenting" by Benjamin Spock, M.D., and Mary Morgan originally appeared in *Experts Advise Parents: A Guide to Raising Loving, Responsible Children*, edited by Eileen Shiff, published by Delacorte Press. Copyright © 1987 by Benjamin Spock, M.D., and Mary Morgan.

Grateful acknowledgment is made to Parade Publications, Inc., for permission to reprint "A Way to Say Farewell" by Benjamin Spock, M.D., which originally appeared in *Parade*, March 10, 1985. Copyright © 1985 by Benjamin Spock, M.D. Reprinted by permission of *Parade*.

# PHOTO CREDITS

**Henri Cartier-Bresson/Magnum:** pp. xv, 138, 158, 166, 172 (all © 1961); **Hella Hammid:** pp. 136, 240; **Library of Congress:** pp. 123, 182, 244; **Morris Rosenfeld:** p. 125; **Pocket Books, a division of Simon and Schuster:** p. 128; **Life/Bob Gomel:** p. 143; **Syracuse University:** p. 169; **New York Post Co., Inc.:** p. 184; **Wendy Wolf:** p. 194; **New York Review of Books:** p. 196 (© 1969 NYRev. Inc.); **AP/Wide World Photos:** pp. xvi, xvii, 205, 217, 266; **Cynthia R. Benjamins:** p. 210; **News Bureau/University of Arkansas at Little Rock:** p. 220; **Gary Speed/Arkansas Gazette:** p. 224; **Judy Spock:** p. 228; © **Jim Kalett:** p. 250 (© 1984); **Lynda Long:** p. 256; **Lionel J-M Delevingne:** p. 265.

# Index

(*Italicized* page numbers refer to photographs.)

Abraham, Karl, 243
Abzug, Bella, *263*, *265*
Adams, Harriett, 10
aging, 253
Agnew, Spiro, *207*
American Indian Movement, 218
Arnaz, Desi, 137
Ashton, Frederick, 140
Auden, W. H., 140

Babcock, Mr., 50–51, *51*, 53, 54–55
*Baby and Child Care* (Spock), 106
   advertisements in, 139
   advertising for, 137
   advice, Spock's approach to,
    241–42
   changes over the years, 242–47
   collaborator for Spock, 248–51
   index to, 152
   longterm effect, 263
   parents' reactions, 135
   "permissiveness" charge against,
    206–7, 263

   publishers' proposals for, 131–33
   publicity for, 137
   purpose of, 135, 262
   reviews from medical profession,
    135–36
   royalties, 137, 139
   sales, 135
   sexism in, 247–48
   Spock's mother and, 17–18,
    136–37
   writing of, 133–35, 152
Bailey, Randy, 147, 148
Ball, Lucille, 137
Bartlett, Dr., (pediatrician), 133
bed-wetting, 246
behavior problems of children,
    parents' responsibility for,
    134–35
Bellevue Hospital (New York City),
   98
Ben Spock Peace Center, 174
Bernbach, William, 167–68
Berrigan, Daniel, 186
Berrigan, Phillip, 186

Bethesda Naval Medical Center, 147–48
Boston Tea Party, 186
Boudin, Kathy, 200
Boudin, Leonard, 200, 208–9
Brazelton, T. Berry, 242, 245–47, 248
breast-feeding, 153–54
Brown, Norton, 99
Bundy, McGeorge, 175
Bunzel, Everett, 105
Butler, William, 171

Caldicott, Helen, *265*
"Call to Resist Illegitimate Authority" (antiwar document), 198–99, 201
Canadian Pacific Railroad, 84–88
*Care and Feeding of Children* (Holt), 25, 35
Chaplin, Charlie, 55, 140–43, *141*
*Chariots of Fire* (film), 79
Charlotte of Luxembourg, Grand Duchess, 162, 163
Chassler, Sey, 223
Cheney, Cynthia, 92, 93
Chomsky, Noam, 192
Citizens' Party, 211
civil disobedience, 185–95, 266
Clark, Ramsey, 209
clergymen in civil disobedience actions, 190–91
Cobb, Clement B. P., 105
Coffin, William Sloane, Jr., 198, 205, *205*, 208, 257
colds in children, 131
Colt, Cynthia, 106
Columbia University College of Physicians and Surgeons, 94, 96, 97–99
Commoner, Barry, 212
communism, American hysteria about, 155–56
Community for Creative Non-Violence, 193–94
compulsive neuroses, 243
Contini, Joe, 84
control of children by parents, 126
Coolidge, Calvin, 96

Coolidge, Mrs. (neighbor of Spock family), 38
Corderry brothers, 71
Cornell Medical College, 100
Councille, Ginger, *232*, 233, 234–38, *236*, *238*
Cousins, Norman, 168, 170, 171
Cushing, Dr., *42*, 50, 54, 55

Debs, Eugene V., 219
De Gaulle, Charles, 163
Dewey, John, 110, 112
Diener, Kenny, *158*
Diener, Linda, *138*
disarmament, 264–66
Doubleday Company, 131–32
Douglas, Helen Gahagan, 171
Douglas, Mike, 75
Duell, Charlie, 137
Dulles, John Foster, 162, 181
Durham University, 140–42
dying, 254–57

eczema in children, 250
education for children, 43–44, 52
Eisenhower, Dwight D., 159, 162, 181
English methods of childraising, 242–43
Erikson, Erik, 39–40, 110
ethics, medical, 256
"experts" on childraising, 133–34

Family Hospital and Clinic (Coronado, Calif.), 152, 153–54
father-son relationships, 16
Federal Bureau of Investigation (FBI), 155, 156, 181
interview with Spock, 197–98, 203
feeding schedules for infants, 124–26
Feigenbaum, Dr., 97
Ferber, Michael, 198, 205
Fieldston School, 119
food for children, 24–25
foot care, 154–55
Foote, Patty, 5, 69
Foote, William, 37
Ford, Francis, 202, 204

Ford, Gerald, 253
Fraad, Lewis, 248
Franco, Francisco, 145
fresh air for children, 242
Freud, Sigmund, 110, 243, 247–48
Friedman, David, 248–49
Frontier College, 84
funerals, 257–58

Gandhi, Mohandas K., 186
Garelik (New York police inspector), 187, 188
Geddes, Donald, 132–33
Gesell (child specialist), 133
Gibson, Langhorn, 71
Ginger (Councille), daughter of Mary Morgan; see under Councille
Ginsberg, Allen, 190
Goldwater, Barry, 174
Goodman, Mitchell, 198, 205
Gould, Mr., 160
grandparents' role in childraising, 126

Hamden Hall (school), 42, 50–56, 56, 58
Hand, Learned, 95
Hanna, Mr., 36
Harrison, Rex, 163
Hayes, Helen, 163
Hershey, General, 209
hippies, 213–14
Hiroshima, bombing of, 155
Ho Chi Minh, 181
Hocking, Professor and Mrs., 45–46
Hoffman, Abbie, 192
Hoffman, Isidore, 171
Holt, Henry, 25, 100–101, 134
Honnedaga Lake, N.Y., 107–8, 107, 108
Hoover, Herbert, 97
Hoover, J. Edgar, 156, 181
Hopkins, Babe, 25
Hopkins Grammar School, 49–50
Horner, Mansfield, 23–24, 28
hospice movement, 257
hospitals, 257
House Un-American Activities Committee (HUAC), 155–56, 171

Hughes, Stuart, 168
Hume, Ted, 70
Humphrey, George, 162

Ilg (child specialist), 133
I Love Lucy (TV show), 137
indictment of Spock, 184, 196, 205
  aftermath, 206–9
  announcement of, 199–200
  appeal of jury decision, 204–5
  background to, 108–00
  defense lawyers, 200–201
  defense strategy, 201–2
  FBI interview, 197–98, 203
  government charges, 201
  press reaction, 205–6
  trial, 202–4

Jack, Homer, 167
Jocelyn, Miss, 46, 47–48
Johnson, Lynda Bird, 164
Johnson, Lyndon, 164–65, 174, 175–76, 181–83
Journal of the American Medical Association, 135–36

Kennedy, Jacqueline, 160–61, 163–64
Kennedy, John, 160, 161–62, 163, 168, 174, 181
Kennedy, Joseph, 181
Kistiakowsky, George B., 175
Kleiner, I., 32
Kludt, Cindy, 229, 231

Ladies Home Journal, 159–60
LaFontaine, Mme., 228–30
Leader, Ed, 72, 73, 74, 74, 75–76, 77–78
Levine, David, 196
Levy, David, 108–9
Lewin, Bertram, 16, 109
Lindley, Al, 71, 78
Lindsay, John, 187
Lion Nine naval hospital, 151–52
longshoremen of New York, 207

McCarthy, Eugene, 247
McCarthy, Joe, 155
McClellan, Jim, 213, 218
McFarland, Bob, 47–48
McLane, Guy, 17, 38
McReynolds, Dave, 186–87
Magidson, Herb, 192, 218
Magidson, Shirley, 218
Marshall, Leonore, 171
masturbation, 60
materialism of Americans, 263–64
May Day 1971 demonstrations (Washington), 191–93
Mead, Margaret, 110
medical education, 112–14
mentally retarded persons in the military, 150
Mitchell, John, 193
Morgan, Mary, *226*, *236*, *250*, *256*, *265*
    civil disobedience actions, 193, 195
    collaborator for Spock, selection of, 249
    courtship, 222–23
    first meeting with Spock, *220*, 221–22
    friendships, 226
    grandmotherly types, love for, 227–30
    health concerns, 259
    personal relationship with Spock, 225–26
    sailing, *224*, 227
    speaking engagements for Spock, arrangement of, 222–23
    stepparent situation in marriage with Spock, 234, 235, 238
    wedding, 223, *224*
*Ms.* magazine, 248

National Conference for New Politics, 172–73
National Women's Political Caucus, 247
Native Americans, 112, 218
New York Hospital-Cornell Medical Center, 105, 101

New York Nursery and Child Hospital, 100–101
New York Psychoanalytic Institute, 109, 110
nuclear power protests, *217*, *265*
Nuremberg Principle, 198–99

Ogden, Miss, 44–45, 59–60
Olympic Games of 1924, 73–79, *76*, *78*
"open-air" school attended by Spock, 45–48, *46*
Ortega, Daniel, *263*

Payne Whitney Clinic, 101–2
Peace and Freedom Party, 222
Peale, Norman Vincent, 206
Pentagon Papers, 198
People's Party, 211, 212–14, 218, 222
"permissiveness" charge against Spock's childraising advice, 206–7, 263
Petrunkevitch, Professor, 37–38
Phillips Academy, 61–62, 63–65
Phoutrides, Aristides, 79
physical punishment of children, 123–24
Pickett, Clarence, 171
Pocket Books Company, 132, 137, 139
Presbyterian Hospital (New York City), 98–100
presidential campaign of 1972:
    cross-country campaigning, 213–15
    election results, 218
    nomination of Spock, 213
    People's Party platform, 212–13
    Secret Service protection, 214–18
    Spock's frustration regarding, 211–12
    Spock's speeches, 211–12
    women's issues, 247
progressive education movement, 110, 112
"project method" of learning, 112–13
psychological aspects of child care, 108–11, 130–31, 242–47, 249

psychological training for pediatricians, 101–2, 109–11
psychopaths in the military, 149

Quarrier, Archie, 75

Rado, Sandor, 109, 145
Ramsey, Peggy, 65, 70, 93
Raskin, Marcus, 198, 202, 204, 213
Rathbone, Basil, 164
*Redbook* magazine, 245
Robbins, Adelaide, 25
Robbins, Chunky, 24–25
Rochester (Minnesota) Child Health Project, 111
Rollins, Jim, 174
Roosevelt, Franklin D., 97
Rothenberg, Jo, 250
Rothenberg, Michael, 249–51, 250
Rusk, Dean, 176–77, 187

St. Alban's naval hospital, 148–51
Salinger, Pierre, 161
"Sandra" (Spock's childhood love interest), 65
SANE (National Committee for a Sane Nuclear Policy), 167–71, 173–74
SANE advertisement of 1962, 167–68, 169
Sanford, Bill, 25–26, 58, 59
San Leandro naval hospital, 152
Sargent, Bill, 25
Sargent, Tom, 25
Schnielock, Marta, 52–53
Seabrook nuclear facility, 217
Secret Service (U.S.), 214–19
Senate Internal Security Committee, 156
Seneca Army Depot protest (1983), 194–95
sex education, 52
sexism, 247–48
Sheldon, Huntington (Ting), 70
*Shoulder Arms* (film), 55
Smith, Al, 97
Snyder, Mitch, 193
sociopaths in the military, 149–51

Spanish Civil War, 145–46
Spock, Anne (sister), 4, 10, 11, 68, 230
Spock, Benjamin Ives (father), 15, 47, 52, 73
   career as lawyer, 8–9
   college years, 17
   courtship of Mildred, 11–12
   death, 17
   European trip, 38, 40
   Maine vacations, 32, 35, 36
   money, attitude toward, 9
   personality, 14
   political views, 96
   relationship with Spock, 14–17, 33–34
   Spock's decision to enter medicine, 92
   Spock's marriage to Jane, 94
Spock, Benjamin McLane, 42, 81, 90, 220, 236, 240, 250, 256, 259
   adolescence, 50–56, 58, 59–60
   advice, approach to, 126, 133–35, 241–42
   on aging, 253
   arrests, 189–90, 189, 191, 192–93, 194–95, 194
   athletic interests, 53–54, 55, 63–64, 64, 71; see also rowing activities *below*
   babysitting, 5
   as "bully" in childhood, 48–49
   camp counselor, 65
   childbirth, early experiences with, 3
   childhood, 2, 3–20, 23–28, 28, 30, 31–40, 39, 44–50, 46
   childhood home, 22
   children of, 117; see also Spock, John; Spock, Michael
   civil disobedience actions, 185–95, 189, 194, 266
   clothing preferences, 51, 88–89, 172, 253–54
   "cocky photo" incident, 38–40, 39
   conscience of, 18
   dancing, 52–53, 62, 73–74
   defiance of mother, 62–63

Spock, Benjamin McLane (*continued*)
Democratic Party affiliation, 97, 162
diet, 258–59
dinners with his parents, 7
on disarmament, 264–66
drafting table, *244*
drowning, fear of, 79
drum-and-bugle corps incident, 55–56
on dying, 254–57
on education for children, 43–44, 52
father, relationship with, 14–17, 33–34
fears and anxieties in childhood, 27–28
fraternity membership, 64–65
friends in childhood, 23–26, 47
funerals, attitude toward, 257–58
grammar school, 44–50
hands of, 222
health problems, 117, 146
high school, 50–56
honorary degree, 140–42, *141*
house visits as pediatrician, 106, 120
as husband, 225–26
indictment for antiwar activities: *see* indictment of Spock
internship, medical, 98–100
left-wing political activities, 172–73; *see also* presidential campaign of 1972
on longevity, 258–59
"long pants" for, 52
Maine vacations as child, 6, 31–40
medical school, 79, 91–92, 94, 97–98, *102*, *114*
military service, *144*, 146–55, *157*
mother's influence on, 17–20
moths, interest in, 26–27
nuclear power protests, *217*, *265*
Olympic appearance, 73–79
orphan girls, interest in, 70–71
as parent, *116*, 117–24
on physical punishment of children, 123–24

political awakening, 95–97
prep school, 61–62, 63–65
presidential bid: *see* presidential campaign of 1972
presidential candidates, endorsements for, 159–62, 174
press conferences, 200
private practice, 105–8, 119–20, 129–31, *132*
psychiatric work, 147–53
psychoanalysis of, 16, 109
psychological training, 101–2, 109–11
railroad work, *82*, 84–88, *85*, *88*
reading, enjoyment of, 44
religious beliefs, 10
residency, medical, 100–102
retirement plans, 207–8
roller skating, 50
romances, school-age and college, 42, 52–53, 59–60, 64, 65–66, 70
rowing activities, 71–79, *74*, 258
safety-pin incident, 99–100
sailing, 34, 79, *122*, 224, 227, 254
as school physician, 106–7
senility, fear of, 255–56
sexism, dealing with, 247–48
sexual interests in youth, 50–51, 52, 54–55
spider-catching incident, 37–38
steamboats, interest in, 33–34
as stepparent, *232*, 233–38
stories, enjoyment of, 24
"summer complaint" as infant, 31
summer pediatric practice, 107–8, *108*
teaching career, 111–12, *138*, 143, *166*
teenagers, advice for, 139
telephone advice, 131
test ban treaty, campaign for, 167–70, *169*
tonsillectomies, 9–10
trains, interest in, 32, 121–23
as undergraduate, *68*, 69–73, 79–80, 91, 96
*Utah* luncheon, 26
Vietnam War protests, 170–72,

175–76, 179–82, *182*, 186–90, 191–93, 198–99; *see also* indictment of Spock
welfare-rights demonstrations, *178*, *210*
White House dinners, 162–65
World War I poster collection, 54
Spock, Betty (sister), 4, 10, 11, *68*, 230
Spock, Bob (brother), 4, 5–6, *8*, *68*, 230, 258
Spock, Dan (grandson), *123*, *228*
Spock, Grandmother, 12
Spock, Jane Cheney (first wife), 60, 120, 146, 147, 161, 243
children of, 117; *see also* Spock, John; Spock, Michael
courtship, 93–94
first meeting with Spock, 92–93
Greenwich Village apartment, 94–95, 99
honeymoon, *90*
as orphan, 70–71
personal relationship with Spock, 225
separation from Spock, 221, 223
Spock's indictment, 199, 200
Spock's presidential bid, 214, 215, 216, 217–18
wedding, 94
White House dinner, 162–63
Spock, John (son), 161, 223, 229, 231
birth, 148
childhood, *121*, 123, 124
on Spock as father, 120–21
Spock, Judy (daughter-in-law), *228*, 230–31
Spock, Marjorie (Hiddy) (sister), 4–5, 10, 11, 44, 62, 230
Spock, Michael (son), 60, 147, *228*, 230
birth and infancy, *116*, 117–18
childhood, 118–19, 120, 121–24
dyslexia, 119
on Spock as father, 120–21
Spock, Mildred Stoughton (mother),

2, 4–5, 6, *8*, *13*, *19*, *20*, 56, 73, 83
*Baby and Child Care* and, 17–18, 136–37
birthings at home, 3
car-driving, 36–37
courtship, 11–12
discipline of her children, 7, 18, 62–63
education for her children, 43, 44
final years, 18–19
health, concerns about, 5
influence on Spock, 17 20
on letter-writing, 133
maids, dealings with, 7–8, 33
Maine vacations, 33, 34, 35, 36
nutrition, views on, 24–25, 35
parents, relations with, 12–14
"peculiar" views, 10–11
perfectability, belief in, 262
photographs of her children, 38–39
religious beliefs, 10
sex, attitude toward, 60–61, 62, 66
Spock's decision to enter medicine, 92
Spock's marriage to Jane, 94
tonsillectomies for Spock, 9–10
Spock, Peter (grandson), *228*
Spock, Sally (sister), 4, *4*, 10, *68*, 94, 230
Spock, Susannah (granddaughter), *228*
Spock, William (brother), 3–4
Steel, Dr., 5
Steichen, Edward, 163
Steinbeck, Mrs. John, 164
Steinem, Gloria, 247–48
Steiner, Claude, 222
stepparenting, 233–38
Stevenson, Adlai, 159
Stoughton, Bradley (uncle), 12, 14
Stoughton, Charles (grandfather), 12–13
Stoughton, Laura (aunt), 13
Stoughton, Leila (aunt), 13
Stoughton, Nanny (grandmother), 11–14, *13*

stress experienced by children, 261
Swanson, Gloria, 75

Taylor, Telford, 202, 205
*Teenager's Guide to Life and Love*
    (Spock), 139
television violence, 249
test ban treaty, campaign for, 167–70
Thomas, Norman, 171
thumb-sucking, 101, 109
*Time* magazine, 248
toilet training, 130, 242–47
Tombs, The (New York detention
    center), 189
Tonkin Gulf Resolution, 176, 198
Treasure Island naval hospital, 152,
    153
Twain, Mark, 127
Tweedy, Helen, 48
Twitchel, Mr., 50, *51*, 52, 53, 54, 55

University of Pittsburgh, 111

Vidal, Gore, 213
Vietnam War, 174–76
    constitutionality question, 198
    protests against, 170–72, 175–76,
        179–82, 186–90, 191–93,
        198–99
Vishno, Charlie, 12
Vishno, Jesamyn, 12

Watson, John, 134
Weir, Mary, 59
Weiss, Cora, 200
welfare-rights demonstrations, *178*,
    *210*
Western Reserve University, 111,
    113, 175
White, E. B., 258–59
Whitehall Street Induction Center
    protest (1967), 186–89, 201
White House Conference on Interna-
    tional Cooperation, 175
White House dinners, 162–65
Wiesner, Jerome, 175, 176
William of Luxembourg, Prince, 162,
    163
Wilson, Al, 71
Wilson, Harold, 164
Women Strike for Peace, 207
Woodbury, Michael, 225
World War I, 24, 54–56
World War II, 145, 146–55
Worthington Hooker School, 45
Wright, Margaret, 214

Yale Medical School, 91–92, 98
Yale University, 50
    rowing team, 71–79, *74*, *78*
    Spock's student days, 69–73,
        79–80, 91, 96

Zachry, Caroline, 43, *104*, 110–11,
    112, 119, 225

# ABOUT THE AUTHORS

BENJAMIN SPOCK, M.D., was born in New Haven, Connecticut, in 1903. He is a contributing editor to *Redbook* and has been writing a regular column for the magazine since 1963. His first book, *Baby and Child Care*, published in 1946, has sold over thirty-nine million copies and has been translated into twenty-six languages. He is also the author of a dozen other books, including *The Problems of Parents*, *Dr. Spock Talks with Mothers*, *Dr. Spock on Vietnam*, *Raising Children in a Difficult Time*, and *Dr. Spock on Parenting*. He has two sons, Michael and John, and five grandchildren.

MARY MORGAN, writer and political activist, is from Esculapia Hollow, Arkansas. She has contributed articles to *Redbook* and *Parade*, as well as to the book *Experts Advise Parents*, edited by Eileen Shiff. She is licensed by the U.S. Coast Guard as a Captain, and currently organizes women's problem-solving groups in Arkansas and Tortola, British Virgin Islands. She has also taught school, worked for the Arkansas State Health Department, and served as a program coordinator for the University of Arkansas Medical School. She has one daughter, Ginger Councille, who lives and works in Los Angeles.

Mary Morgan and Benjamin Spock were married in 1976, and now live aboard their sailboat *Carapace* in Tortola in the winter, and aboard the twenty-three-foot sloop *Turtle* in Maine in the summer.